FRISBEE

by the Masters

FRISBEE
by the Masters

Charles Tips

Photographs by Mike Fluitt

Drawings by Byron Sewell

 CELESTIAL ARTS
Millbrae, California

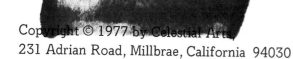
Editing: Holly Carver
Composition: Ann Hidalgo Manley
Paste-up: Cathy Lenox, Cindy Fluitt

First printing: March, 1977
Made in the United States of America

Library of Congress Cataloging in Publication Data

Tips, Charles, 1949–
    Frisbee by the masters

    1. Frisbee (Game) I. Title.
GV1097.F7T56   796.2   76-55832
ISBN: 0-89087-142-6

2 3 4 5 6 7 8 – 82 81 80 79 78 77

To Terry, James, and Ed, and the other great players out on the mall for all the wonderful hours, and to Lois for all the wonderful years.

We find, upon climbing past the higher branches, that we all can fly.

—Richard Fariña

Contents

Foreword

There is something special about the Frisbee disc. It seems simple enough—a plastic saucer. It can be propelled in an incredible number of methods, fly in a wide range of trajectories and attitudes, and be caught in an infinite number of methods. The catch is particularly intriguing because it makes maximum use of the flight characteristics of the disc. When freestyle experts catch a saucer, they rarely hold it on initial contact but rather play with the flight of the disc for several moments before stopping its rotation in the final catch. This can involve such things as changing flight attitude through touching the surface of the disc; adding or reducing rotation; or using the spin to carom off body parts, all while taking into account the flow of the wind, which has a profound effect on the whole operation. All this requires an intimate knowledge of the nature of the Frisbee disc's flight. Careless or gross contact in flight can produce wobbly, unpredictable gyrations. The triumph comes in co-operating with the saucer in the production of the desired result.

One of the amazing features of the disc, however, is that pleasures are available at all levels of competence. Just to see it fly through the brightness of a summer afternoon can bring a special joy all its own. The inexpert catcher leaps and merely grazes the bottom of the disc, and amazingly it glides up into the wind and returns to be caught again. The ball holds no such mystery. It has a slavish attachment to the Earth and falls quickly if missed in the first catching attempt. Frisbee holds a special wonder. It responds clearly to its treatment and is almost eager to perform.

This amazing toy wonder has generated an especially interesting impact on its admirers. The Frisbee disc was a smash hit when introduced. It was popular in fad dimensions. People loved the way it flew, the way it curved and soared. As with all fads, the wide appeal of the original Pluto Platter fell off. Most people moved on to the next interesting toy, but a few continued to play with the disc, having had a glimpse of its possibilities. As they continued, these early enthusiasts learned more about the saucer and developed activities utilizing that new knowledge. Progress was slow. Each little pocket of enthusiasm made its own breakthroughs, depending on its mix of personality and creativity. They advanced, but there was much to learn.

The establishment of the International Frisbee Association in 1967 was the first significant response to the scattering of continuing interest which existed. The critical flow of information had begun. More than any sports, Frisbee play allows and requires discovery. It is a giant task for any individual. Communication and its power of collective creativity open the possibilities. Along with the opening of communication came the first sharing of games. Players other than the original creators began to play the Frisbee games and began to use techniques others had developed. As this exchange grew in volume, the "learning curve" of Frisbee play began to rise. During this period there was little direct contact between players. The only major opportunity was the International Frisbee Tournament held annually in the Upper Peninsula of Michigan. Primarily a guts tournament, the event brought an increasingly large number of players together. The I.F.T. gradually responded to the broadening interests of the players, first including distance (1962) and then accuracy (1967) and MTA (1973).

In 1974, however, the explosion of development began with the advent of major tournaments in Michigan, New Jersey, and Toronto which drew players from a wide area. These contacts, combined with improved communication, generated advances in all aspects of the sport, culminating with the first World Championship, in California. 1975 brought continued growth for all the meets and, after the '75 W.F.C., the I.F.A. was revamped to accommodate the growing needs of the membership and the sport. Resulting from this reorganization were three major developments which added

to and consolidated this spiraling interest.

The National Championship Series: Hosted by clubs across the country, events feature competition which both qualifies players for the World Championship and provides opportunity for informal exchange. The season runs from March to August, ending with the World Frisbee Championship meet held annually in Los Angeles. In general, the meets are open to all comers, with some requiring preregistration. The schedule of meets is published in *Frisbee World*.

Frisbee World: The most important feature of the current I.F.A. program, this magazine reports on event results, technique, records, club activities, and other information of interest to the enthusiast.

Affiliate Clubs: The heart of the I.F.A., the affiliate program supports the development of these clubs by providing various informational services and aiding in the attraction of new membership. Most people make their major advancements in the local club. The groups range in organizational complexity from those who have extensive programs of activity, including local newsletters and competitions, to very informal operations which consist only of an occasional get-together to play.

The impact of these programs has been substantial. In terms of performance, the results may best be viewed through the records set in the first year of the Series. All the men's, women's, and seniors' event records except one were bettered during the year's competition. This kind of advancement is indication of the infancy of Frisbee play as a sport. The combination of information flow and the influx of new talent promises to produce many years of similar progress. It is this promise that is attractive to new players. In few sports can one actually be innovative. Championship Frisbee play demands that creativity and should for a very long time to come. It is quite conceivable that a first-year tournament player could introduce a new move to freestyle. Few other sports hold such a possibility.

The organizational progress of Frisbee play obviously has many benefits. It also holds some threats. Overformalization could harm the spontaneity of play. Overemphasis on competition could make the disc another example of our ability to take the fun out of essentially joyful activity. Protection of these joys is a major goal of the I.F.A. Formal competition is encouraged but, even on that level of play, emphasis is placed on quality of experience, not competitive results. Teams play to win, but within the context of an alternative standard of behavior. The spirit of the game statement for ultimate Frisbee has been stated as follows:

Ultimate Frisbee has traditionally been considered an alternative athletic activity. Highly competitive play is encouraged but never at the expense of the bond of mutual respect between players or the basic joy of play. Protection of these vital elements removes some types of "sport" behavior from the Ultimate field. Such actions as taunting of opposition players, dangerous aggression, intentional fouling or other "win at all costs" behaviors are fouls against the spirit of the game and should be discouraged by all players.

The body of Frisbee enthusiasts have often been called the Frisbee family. The choice of this term reflects the special nature of Frisbee play. It is naturally co-operative, complimentary, and encourages mutual support. That spirit not only makes Frisbee play a uniquely pleasurable activity, but also serves as an example to other sports in which the essential exhilaration of play has been forgotten.

The intent, therefore, of all structured Frisbee activity is not to model after other sport structures but rather to enhance each individual's ability to maximize pleasure with the disc. Frisbee play is sport—a sport for the fun of it.

Within the pages of *Frisbee by the Masters* are the keys to the flying disc's potential. Charles has assembled this body of information through careful study and the contribution of many players. It represents the history of almost thirty years of human discovery. Each technique is a challenge in itself. To read of a particular skill in these pages is only the beginning of a learning and adapting process through which players make the techniques their own. Every new player brings new style to every move. Few athletic activities reflect individual differences as profoundly as Frisbee play. As novices learn, they add to the text through their own impact. Those of us who have sketched the outline look forward eagerly to those additions and welcome our new co-authors.

—Stork

Dan Roddick
Director
International Frisbee
  Association

Acknowledgments

This book gets its title from the fact that many expert Frisbee players have contributed to it. The players I have corresponded with for advice and information are Alan Blake, Tom Bodá, Jo Cahow, Mike Conger, Patti Hipsky, Irv Kalb, Rick Kauvar, Kerry Kolmar, Monika Lou, Tom McRann, Victor Malafronte, Tom Monroe, José Montalvo, Don Pierce, Dan Roddick, and Ken Westerfield. Their help has been invaluable.

I have learned the things I know about the disc from playing with, speaking with, and watching many, many people; a list would be impossible. I would like, however, to thank the following players for their good advice and helpful pointers during the last couple of years: Steve Gottlieb, Ed Headrick, John Kirkland, Gail McColl, and Paul Thompson. Marc Reischman, Jim Baumann, Danny McInnis, and Jim Howard have been of particular help, as have many others here in Texas.

Two books on the disc have been published before this one, *Frisbee: A Practitioner's Manual and Definitive Treatise* by Dr. Stancil E. D. Johnson (Workman Publishing Company, 1975) and *The Official Frisbee Handbook* by Goldy Norton (Bantam Books, 1972). Both are very different from other sports books because Frisbee play is different from other sports, and both authors were clever enough to capture the unique charm of Frisbee in their books. Even though this book presents Frisbee in a more straightforward light than have the other two books, I hope you will find something of the free spirit of Frisbee play in this book too. I want to acknowledge my great debt to my two predecessors, not just for hours of absorbing reading, but for the insights I have stolen from their books. I enthusiastically recommend both books to you if you are one of those few players who hasn't already read them.

Repeated thanks goes to Patti Hipsky, Jo Cahow, and Dan Roddick for the assistance they have given from the offices of the International Frisbee Association. Likewise, Jim Kerrigan and Dick Gillespie at Wham-O have supplied me with information I would not have had otherwise. Larry Abraham helped me to better understand the mechanics of throwing and catching, and Jay Shelton and Herman Matthews helped me to understand that I will probably never understand the physics of saucer flight (the Frisbee disc is very complex aerodynamically). Hal Kramer and his staff at Celestial Arts have given all the support and enthusiasm any author could ever hope for from a publisher.

I owe an extremely large debt of gratitude to four people who have labored hard on the production of this book: Rich Hendel, Holly Carver, Cindy Fluitt, and Ann Manley. I doubt I would have undertaken this book if I had not known I could count on their help.

And a special thanks to Sam and Janet.

Photos by Gary Gossett

Introduction

Frisbee play has acquired many specialized terms and concepts over the years, and I have had to add a few of my own for the sake of clarity and brevity. Also, many of the constant characteristics of Frisbee play are described here to spare continual repetition. This introduction condenses into a few pages things that would normally be learned over a period of months, so, particularly if you are new to Frisbee, you are likely to find a number of things in this section that will only begin to make good sense as you gain playing experience. Read now and refer back often.

I have used three shortcuts in my writing that you need to be aware of. (1) Any reference that could apply to more than one part of the body should be taken to mean the part most directly involved in handling the disc. For instance, "Keep the elbow in close" should be taken to refer to the elbow of the throwing arm (or catching arm, whichever is pertinent). (2) Throwing ranges have been estimated for players who can, standing flat-footed, comfortably throw a backhand farther than thirty meters. Most players over the age of twelve should

be capable of reaching that distance. (Krae Van Sickle set a junior distance record of 93 yards at the age of fifteen.) If you are a short-range thrower, adjust the recommended ranges accordingly. (3) As you have already noticed, I mix my units of measurements to suit myself. If you are not familiar with the metric system, figure ten meters to eleven yards and five centimeters to two inches. That'll get you more than close enough, since I usually use metric for approximations.

THE FRISBEE DISC

Properly, the term Frisbee can only be used to describe discs made by Wham-O Mfg. Co., which is all right since Wham-O manufactures sport-quality discs. Discs made by other manufacturers, except for one or two borderline cases, simply do not perform well enough to be worth considering for general use.

I recommend any of three discs for all-around play: the Super-Pro, the 119 G, and the 141 G (the "G" stands for "grams"). After that, the Pro (including close cousins the All-American and the Moonlighter), the 165 G, the 97 G, and the Master can be used for all-around play but are favored more for special performance qualities. The Fastback is regaining popularity and may one day be on the market again, and the Mini-Frisbee is always popular for indoor (and outdoor) play. The Regular model is the best for young children.

Each model has somewhat different flight characteristics, as do discs of the same model but from different molds—even though they are identical in appearance! Such passionate arguments rage about which are the better models and mold numbers that I think I will avoid drawing fire and simply say try them all. You'll probably want them all in your Frisbee golf bag anyway. Stancil Johnson provides an excellent performance table for more than fifty types of discs, begining on page 202 of his book. You may want to refer to it. But keep in mind that his ratings were made before Wham-O launched the World Class Series ("G" Series) and that most players rate World Class discs higher than the top-ranked Super-Pro.

The life expectancy of your disc is somewhere between two minutes and twenty years, depending on how you treat it. Some Pluto Platters (one of the very earliest models) that have received loving care are still in use. Soap, water, and a bristle brush will keep your disc clean, and steel wool and fine sandpaper will keep the surface free of nicks and scratches. However, some advanced techniques can suffer if the disc is blemished at all. Many top players use a disc only a few times before turning it over to the practice pile.

Play with a quality disc in good condition or you will be putting unnecessary handicaps in the way of learning. Once you are a proficient player, you might better appreciate the flight peculiarities of toy discs during occasional experimentation. You can also experiment with plastic and paper plates, garbage can lids, coffee can lids, pie pans, and many other disclike objects. When I worked at sea, I used to have the bo's'n save paint can lids for me so I could practice my throws without any worry of a stray gust carrying a Frisbee irretrievably over the side.

The names for the parts of the disc that you will need to be familiar with are shown in the diagram. The only comment I have is that logically there is no top and bottom, and certainly no upside down, to a disc. However, the terms are well established, and I couldn't come up with any replacements that were any clearer.

THE FRISBEE PLAYER

A way has come about in Frisbee terminology to avoid repeatedly specifying right and left side, and thank goodness since Frisbee is a more ambidex-

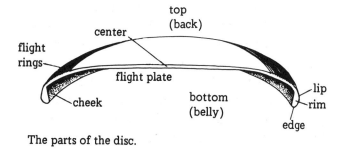

The parts of the disc.

trous sport than most. *Onside* refers to the side of the body handling the disc. The other side is the *offside*. Any time the onside arm makes a throw or catch on the offside, it is said to be *cross-body*. Anything else I have to say about the body should be readily understandable, except that I have had to be particularly specific on names for parts of the hand. A diagram is provided.

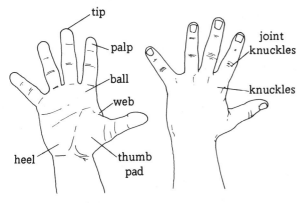

The parts of the hand.

Let me draw your attention in the diagram to the term "palp," which I have borrowed from *The Game of Table Tennis* by Dick Miles. Many grips and discwork techniques would be difficult to describe without a way to distinguish between the very tip of the finger and the fleshy pad beneath, where the fingerprint is. Palp refers to the latter.

THROWING AND CATCHING

The Frisbee exists for one purpose only: to fly. That begins with the throw, which begins with the grip. Any way you can hold the disc you can throw it. Beyond that, make sure you are getting comfortable firmness in your grips (usually, just enough to indent the flight plate slightly) and experiment with the different grips until you develop a feel for them.

There are two basic grips: the fan grip and the two-finger grip. The fan grip is used for the backhand grip (with the thumb on top of the disc) and the overhand-wrist-flip grip (with the thumb under the disc). The two-finger grip is used for the sidearm grip (with the thumb on top of the disc) and the hook-thumber grip (with the thumb under the disc). Notice that if discs had a second flight plate, covering the bottom so that they were uniform like a discus, only the two basic grips, not all four, would be possible. There are endless variations of these four grips, and there are many other grips not so closely related (see chapters 6 and 7).

If you ever hope to play with a smooth flow between catch and throw, you have to develop a feel for the relationship between the grips. Here is a way to learn the six major grips and their relationships at the same time (there are pictures of these grips at the beginning of their respective chapters if you get lost): make a fist. Place a disc into your fist so that the thumb is on top and the fingertips all touch the cheek. The forefinger should hook snugly around the edge. That is the fist grip, a backhand grip that is rapidly gaining popularity. Next, stand the disc up in your hand, put your forefinger on the lip, and fan the other fingers out. That is the classic backhand grip. Slide the disc down into the web of your hand and shift it until it is clenched between the ring finger on the lip and the middle finger on the cheek. This is the sidearm grip.

Pivot the disc on the web of the hand so that the thumb and middle finger exchange places. That is the hook-thumb grip. Roll the disc back down into your palm until the thumb is on the cheek and the forefinger is on the rim. That is the wrist-flip grip. Now, fold the disc down over the thumb pad. You're back into a fist-grip position, except that the thumb is on the cheek and the fingers are on top (just below the flight rings is best). That is the thumber grip.

I am repeatedly asked how many different throws there are. But the question is impossible to answer. Obviously, no two throws are alike, just as you never sign your name the same way twice. In that sense there have certainly been more than one hundred billion different throws. If you want to categorize throws on the basis of variations in grip, delivery angle, stance, speed of rotation or flight, and so forth, then there are hundreds or even thousands of different throws. The idea is not to think in terms of fixed categories but in terms

of the unlimited possibilities. My own feeling is that there are tremendous discoveries yet to be made in Frisbee play, and they will not be made by anyone looking to master only a set number of techniques.

Still, if we are to communicate our disc discoveries, we must have categories to refer to for convenience. Throws have customarily been categorized first by grip. The throwing families discussed in this book are differentiated according to grip. Within each family, the various throws are characterized by the stance from which they are delivered and the angle of delivery. The thrower faces square to the target in the *facing stance* and faces away from the target in the *blind stance*. The facing stance is not so common for throws but is a common catching stance. The blind stance is used for numerous trick throws and catches. The two main throwing stances are the *open stance* and the *closed stance*. The open stance is used for forehanded throws (the name comes from the fact the arm is opened away from the body in the cocked throwing position). The closed stance, which gets its name for the opposite reason, is used for backhands. They are not called simply forehand stance and backhand stance because too many other types of throws are delivered from them.

Stance is not that important a concept for catching, but *set up* is. To set up is to get in position to make whatever catch you want to as the disc approaches. Set-up is also the name for spinning the disc up into the air horizontally. It is such a handy practice technique that I'd suggest, if you don't already know it, you turn to the beginning of chapter 13 and learn it before anything else.

A catch is any method of arresting the disc's flight, but a true catch is made in the "C" of the hand, that is, between the thumb and fingers. Any other way of arresting the disc's flight is a *trap*. Techniques that manipulate the disc's flight without arresting it are known as *discwork*.

Some other throwing terms: *reach* is the distance from the cap of the shoulder to the center of the disc. The *stroke* is the delivery from the time the hand starts forward until release—minus the backswing, that is. A *cuff* is a grip with the non-throwing hand (usually), used to steady the disc during the stroke. (If both hands impart spin to the disc at release, that is a two-handed throw, not a cuffed throw.)

Some customary abbreviations for throwing and catching positions: Between the legs becomes *btl*. Behind the back becomes *btb*. And behind the head is *bth*. Overhand wrist flip shortens to *owf*.

FLIGHT

The disc gets some new names once it is airborne. The flight plate is divided into quarters. The forward quarter is the *nose*. On either side of the nose are the *shoulders*. The last quarter is the *tail*. The shoulder that spins forward is called the *skip shoulder*, because, when it is the first part of the disc to touch down, the disc will *skip* (take off up into the air again), or at least try to, depending on what the landing surface is like and how much flight momentum is left. The other shoulder is called the *roll shoulder*, because, when it is the first part of the disc to touch down, the disc will roll, or, again, at least try to.

Notice that these designations don't change with the spin of the disc, that is, the nose doesn't turn around and around with the spin. However, they are not necessarily constant throughout the disc's flight. For instance, in a *boomerang* flight (the flight you get when the disc is thrown outward and upward, usually into the wind, so that it stalls and glides back toward the thrower), when the disc starts back the tail becomes the nose and vice versa, and the skip shoulder and roll shoulder switch too.

Spin direction, however, is unalterable. Spin is the rotation of the disc around the spin axis (see the diagram of disc axes); it gives gyroscopic stability to the disc's flight. Obviously, spin can go in either of two directions, and, once the disc takes on one spin, it can't go in the other until after it has been brought to a standstill. Imagine a vertical plane through the disc's flight axis. If the skip shoulder is to the thrower's right of the plane (when the thrower is facing in the direction of the throw), the disc is said to have *right spin*. Conversely, the disc is said to have *left spin* when the skip shoulder

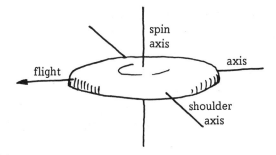

Flight axes.

is to the left. That holds true whether the disc is flying rightside up or upside down (yes, the disc flies perfectly well upside down), even though that means that if the disc turns over past vertical (around the flight axis) right spin becomes left and vice versa. That is as it should be because what is important is not the absolute spin but the way the disc will move on impact with the ground or with the catcher's hand or body.

If you're still not clear on spin, think of it this way: with a few easily recognizable exceptions, any time a left-hander throws from a closed stance or a right-hander throws from an open stance, the disc will carry right spin. The converse is true for left spin. If you're still not clear on spin, don't worry; it only really matters for advanced catching and discwork, and, by the time you're at that stage, spin will be second nature.

I've already mentioned boomerang flights, skip and roll flights, and upside-down flights. The type of flight you get depends primarily on the angle of delivery. Every type of flight is possible within each family of throws. Check the diagram of delivery angles here in the introduction and also at the beginnings of chapters 2 through 5. Two other very important types of flight are the *hover*, or *floater*, and the curve flights. Hovers are thrown about halfway between a level throw and a boomerang so that they level out as they stall out. Any extra spin

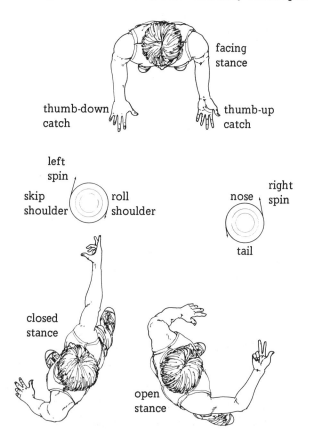

(overspin) you can give the disc at release will help prevent your hover from *sliding* off (also known as fading) prematurely.

There are four basic kinds of curve flight: *skip curves* are thrown with the arm in a lowered position. They get their name from the fact that the skip shoulder is the lowest point of the disc during flight, and so they would tend to skip on contact with the ground. Roll curves are thrown with the arm in a raised position, and they get their name from the fact that they would roll if they were to land. There are also upside-down roll curves and skip curves.

If you consider banks different from curves, as I do, then there are eight different flights. I consider a curve to be a flight that travels in a steady arc with one shoulder inclined higher than the other. Banks, on the other hand, have a noticeable peak in mid-flight and have a greater incline from nose to tail than from shoulder to shoulder. Upside-down roll banks pancake (flatten out) into very graceful lobs.

I should mention that my names for curve flights do not conform to current accepted terminology— my only major departure. Commonly, curves are referred to as "right" and "left." However, one group holds that "right" and "left" pertain to the direction of curve at the beginning of the throw; a second group holds that they pertain to the end of the throw. To show you how far the confusion goes, Stancil Johnson claims on page 62 of his book that the terms refer to the direction the flight turns at the end. Directly beneath that claim is a diagram that shows just the opposite. The terms "normal" (for a curve that goes to the thrower's right side, as a right-hander's backhand skip curve) and "reverse" (for a curve that goes to the thrower's left) are becoming standard, but they lack useful descriptiveness. Besides, who's to say what's normal?

Turnover is a common problem for beginners, a result of throwing with too much arm and too little wrist. The greater the momentum and the less the spin, the greater the turnover. However, to some extent, turnover is a built-in property of any disc. In some disc models it is almost negligible; in others it is considerable or even uncontrollable. If you want to see real turnover, throw a paper plate. The turnover in Wham-O discs always involves the skip shoulder lifting (in upside-down flights, lift is downward), as is the case with almost every flying disc. There are a very few discs, though, that lift at the roll shoulder. The tendency of the disc to turn over is compensated for in the delivery by *hyzer*. Hold the disc at the exact angle you want it to fly, then angle the skip shoulder slightly away from the direction it will lift. That adjustment is the hyzer. Also, hyzer is often used simply to mean the angle of delivery. The various illustrations of delivery angles should give you a good picture of what hyzer is all about.

Turnover may be a demon for beginners, but,

once it is mastered, it is a very handy extra dimension of the disc's flight, responsible for some of the most beautiful features of flight. One type of flight that depends on exaggerated turnover is the *barrel-roll*. With the arm kept fairly straight and with little wrist action, a good, hard throw can turn over 180° or more, depending on the model of the disc and the style of delivery (hook-thumb sidearms work great).

Similar to the barrel-rolls are the *gym-floor curves*, which are skips standing too nearly vertical to take off. So, they just skither crazily across the ground,

The angles of release. (a) multiple skip, (b) skip, (c) level flight (would tend to slide on contact with the ground), (d) dishing (skims around and around on its edge when it hits the ground), (e) crescent roll (the disc would curve sharply to the right, in this case, on landing, (f) veer roller (would angle off to the right on landing), (g) straight roller, (h) curve roller (would curve off to the left), (i) upside-down flight (would tend to slide on contact with the ground), (j) water skip (for skipping the disc across water), (k) back skip (the disc pops up into a gym-floor curve), (l) gym-floor curve (skithers across the ground in an "S" pattern, in this case). The gap between "h" and "i" comes from the fact that the back of the disc lacks an edge to keep the disc from simply collapsing into a slide. Notice that in each case the skip shoulder will be the edge furthest from the hand and that the lift will be operating counterclockwise on the skip shoulder as viewed in this diagram. For example, see the hyzer adjustment for a level flight in "c." Needless to say, ground features play a large role in the way a disc behaves on landing.

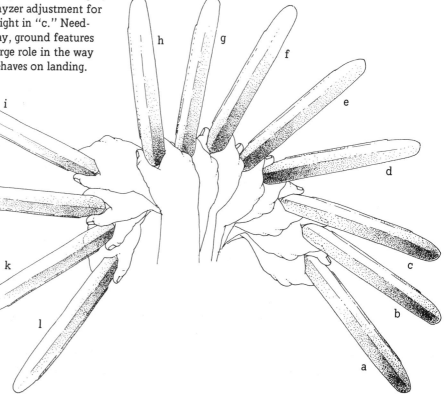

in four basic patterns—"C," "?," "S," and "↻"—depending on the style of delivery used. Give a little whippier release than you would to a barrel-roll because the friction between the skip shoulder and the ground can quickly kill the spin. In fact, they get their name from the fact that a gym floor is the ideal surface for them—minimum friction. You may be surprised to learn that gym-floor curves are tremendously accurate, even apart from the fact that it is impossible to overshoot your target with one.

One other flight I'll mention is the *water skip*, an upside-down flight thrown so that the back of the skip shoulder hits down first—very handy for skimming the disc over the water.

Some types of flights require a change in the disc's attitude. With *positive attitude*, the nose is up and the belly is taking some of the force of the throw; it's like putting on the brakes (see chapter 8). *Negative attitude* jacks the tail up so wind can get under the disc (see chapter 9). The attitude is neutral when the nose and tail are moving on the same plane, whether the disc is level, climbing, banking, or whatever. Only when the belly or back of the disc are tilted into the throw does the disc have positive or negative attitude on it.

In a looser sense, attitude means whatever angle the disc happens to be in. While it is not important in this sense for describing the flight of the disc (terms like climb and curve are more specific), it is important in discwork, where more specific terms are just starting to evolve. Often in discwork, being able to make subtle adjustments in the attitude of the disc is crucial to the setting up of the steps that follow.

An incredible number of factors influence the flight of a Frisbee disc. As one physicist told me, "We can land a spaceship on Mars, but Science doesn't yet understand exactly why a Frisbee flies as it does." The really amazing thing is how quickly a person can bring all those factors under control to produce an unlimited variety of flights at will.

WHERE TO PLAY

Many Frisbee players consider Lower Sproul on the University of California at Berkeley campus to be to Frisbee what New Orleans is to jazz. A few years back, I was standing in a small plaza at Berkeley asking directions to Lower Sproul, when I was told I was standing in the middle of it. Well, it certainly wasn't the wide open spaces of Texas, but I've found out that's not so important. Pick a place that will give you a challenge. A hedge to make leaping catches over; a tree to bank throws around; a hard, bald spot in the grass to make skip shots tricky; a nearby wall for wall rollers and skips—that's what you want, not some dull, vacant field.

Mobile play has been tried on ice skates, snow skis, roller skates, motorcycles, and bicycles. The Frisbee and the bicycle blend into beautiful harmony. What a fantastic sensation to coast in under the flying disc to make your catch! Water play offers dimensions you never find on land. Throwing from an inner tube or air mattress is a trick in itself.

You can play games anywhere. When a Frisbee player retires for the evening, no matter how small the room, there's still room to practice tipping and delays. By the time this book is published, John Kirkland will probably have fulfilled his dream of playing Frisbee across the World Trade Towers in New York City. With imagination, you can turn any place into a Frisbee field. Of course, what you look for in a playing area may depend on what game you want to play.

WHAT TO PLAY

Freestyle is what Frisbee play is all about—two people keeping the disc moving back and forth. More and more, the emphasis is on stylistic complexity and the development of rhythm and dance-like movements. Freestyle is sometimes judged in tournament competition. A variation of freestyle in which two or more players work together at one end or both ends to do fancy discwork is known as *co-oping.*

Guts was an early development. It is a David-and-Goliath game that involves two teams of five (usually, but fewer will do) alternating turns at trying to shred each other with powerful and cunning throws. The teams face each other over a battleground fourteen meters long. The width of the field is determined by the line up of the players; it is the total width of their outstretched arms—fingertips to fingertips. A throw anywhere outside the reach of the catching team (they are not required to jump, but if they do, the throw is judged good or bad on the basis of the reach while jumping) earns a point for the catching team. No point is awarded on a throw that is caught cleanly (the disc may be bobbled and batted, and it may be caught simultaneously by more than one player, but no player may use anything more than one hand to make the catch).

The throwing team gets a point if the disc is trapped or missed. First team to twenty-one wins, but must win by two. Whichever player catches the Frisbee then throws it. On a drop, whichever player touched it first throws it. An ace is a throw that zips through the line untouched. It's a very satisfying accomplishment for the thrower, but it also means that the opponent's most potent thrower may be given the disc to throw back at you.

Ultimate is a field game for two seven-person teams, traditionally played on a field sixty yards long and forty yards wide with thirty-yard end zones. Points are scored by successfully passing the disc to a teammate already in the end zone. You can't run in for a score. In fact, a player who makes a running catch has only three steps to come to a halt. After that, the player may pivot on one foot but may only advance the disc by passing it to a teammate. However, any player who gets possession of the disc behind the goal line being defended may elect to walk the disc straight to the goal line before passing.

Possession changes whenever a pass hits the ground, is intercepted, or goes out of bounds, or when a disc is dropped during a catching attempt (but only during a catching attempt). If the player with the disc has not passed by the time a defensive player has called "stalling" and has counted aloud to fifteen, possession goes over. Any player on the team gaining possession may pick up the disc and play it from where it is or from where it went across the goal line or out of bounds. Only one player may guard the player with the disc. After a point is scored, teams switch ends, line up on the goal lines, and the scoring team throws off to start play again. Play continues through two twenty-four minute halves.

Golf, like guts, is a game that goes way back in Frisbee history. There's no telling how many thousands of courses around the country have been played using such things as lampposts and fireplugs as the targets to "hole out" on. In 1974, a formal course was laid out in Oak Grove Park in La Cañada, California. Shortly after that, Ed Headrick designed a very clever standardized target, the Disc Pole Hole (see page 48). Since then, disc golf and the Disc Pole Hole have spread like wildfire, with Frisbee golf courses being installed in parks and school yards all across the country.

Disc golf is similar to ball golf as far as rules go. (Frisbee players refer to "golf," meaning "disc golf," and "ball golf," meaning the kind played with sticks and pimply balls.) The one disc golf rule you should know is that fairway throws are made with the foot closest to the hole planted on the spot where the disc came to rest. You'll find, however, that disc-golf strategy is more complex than ball-golf strategy, because of the limitless flight possibilities of the disc, assuming your course is sufficiently tough.

The Frisbee field events, more than anything else, probe the relationship of the disc to its natural environment—wind and air. The *distance* event requires working knowledgeably with the elements to get the longest possible ride for your throw. *Accuracy* with a disc is not as simple as it is with a ball; balls don't interact much with the air. In accuracy throwing, a Frisbee player must take into account one hundred and one little things breeze can do to the disc.

The official tournament target for accuracy is two medium-sized Hula Hoops joined together to make one, set up so that the bottom of the target is three feet off the ground. The official procedure is to have each contestant make four throws from each of seven different throwing stations—three straight in front of the target at fifteen, twenty-five, and thirty-five yards, and stations at fifteen and twenty-five yards on each of two lines, 70° on opposite sides of the straight line.

MTA (maximum time aloft) is the attempt to harness all the forces of the wind to keep your disc airborne for as long as possible. However, before the throw can be counted, it must be caught cleanly in one hand—no traps. Ken Westerfield currently holds the world record with a toss that stayed up fifteen seconds. *TR&C* (throw, run, & catch) requires incredible tightroping of the disc—getting it to cover a lot of ground, and then to fall off keeping just the right angle, at just the right moment and in just the right direction so you can make your catch as far as possible from the spot where you launched it in the first place. John Kirkland holds the world record at 234 feet.

I have sketched out these games and contests so that, if you weren't aware of them, you will at least have some idea of how they are played and how to play them yourself. The International Frisbee Association can provide you with complete, up-to-date rules and information for all the games. Write Box 664, Alhambra, California 91802. Disc-golf rules and information on setting up a disc-golf course in your community are available from the Disc Golf Association, Box 866, La Cañada, California 91011.

A fairly complete description of an MTA flight

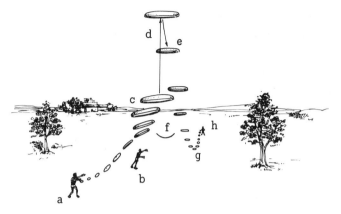

The direction of the wind is into the page. An MTA throw. (a) the throw (in this case with right spin; left spin would involve a throw from the right side of the diagram to the left), (b) running to get in position for the catch, (c) shelfing and possible helixing, (d) towering, (e) drift, (f) fall-off angle, (g) platforming and possible inflection points, (h) the catch.

(accompanied by the diagram), however, will demonstrate how truly complex the field events are and will provide an opportunity to acquaint you with more flight terms. Most players throw MTA with either a backhand or a sidearm skip curve. The throw is made into the wind so that the disc *shelfs* (stalls with the nose just slightly up) at about the widest part of its curve. After it shelfs, a disc will often *helix*, wobble a couple of times in a motion very similar to dishing. What you hope for at that point is that the disc will *tower*, an amazing phenomenon in which the disc shoots straight up in the air. The upward tilt of the nose becomes the upward tilt of the tail as the disc falls off and glides back the other way.

Normally, you try to play the disc to fall off at a slight angle away from the incoming flight, so that the flight will cover more distance, but not so much that you can't run it down for the catch. If conditions are right, before the disc falls off it can drift in a negative attitude a short way. Soon, however, the disc noses back for the ground. If you make your catch at that point, you can get a respectable time. However, depending on the steepness of the descent, the force of the breeze, and the angle of disc to the breeze, the disc can *platform*, that is, tend to level out. Obviously, the disc will go farther that way, and the flight will slow down as well. After platforming, you might also get *inflection points*, little air hops that add time and distance to the flight.

With a long, slow helix; a tall tower; good drift; just the right fall-off angle; a shallow angle of descent; an early platform; some inflection points; and a catch made just inches above the ground, you can start looking for a world-record time.

BEGINNING PRACTICE

The first objective of practice at the beginning level should be to transport the different throwing and catching techniques from the level of the reading mind down to the level where physical skill learning takes place. Read just enough to get a general idea of the movement involved in the particular trick you want to learn. And, if you can learn any of the different tricks just from the illustrations or photographs without having to read about them at first, so much the better. Let's put it this way: the human ability to imitate anything that can be visualized goes back millions of years. The ability to learn by reading step-by-step instructions goes back only a few hundred years.

Generally, you are going to have to have someone to play with, and the buddy system is the best way to start out anyway. You and your playing buddy should pick two to four new techniques to work on each time you play—one or two throws and one or two catches (wait a while before getting into discwork). Make a stab at doing the whole trick at once, and, if you get even a crude approximation of what the technique should be or do, set the book aside and just play. If your first attempt seems totally wrong, check the book again to make sure you haven't overlooked some essential feature of the technique. Trust your body to correct any errors without your trying to figure out what the problem is. Especially, don't be concerned about inaccuracy or wobble in your throws. They'll improve.

There are, however, three mistakes beginners sometimes make that can significantly hamper progress and that should be pointed out and corrected as soon as it becomes obvious that any one of them is going to persist: (1) the tendency to move too early to make a trick catch, (2) the tendency to roll the wrist over during the stroke, and (3) failure to make hyzer adjustments.

If your throws are turning over, you are either rolling your wrist, not throwing with the right hyzer, or both. Both problems are somewhat common in sidearms and overhand wrist flips. In an overhand wrist flip, rolling the wrist is sometimes referred to as "skying" the fingers, since the fingers point upward at release. I find the best way to correct both problems is to stand next to the player and lay my forearm just over the correct path of the stroke, so that the disc will hit my forearm if the throw is made incorrectly. Once the error is corrected in that manner, I have the player drill on it a good while to make sure it stays corrected. If you notice either of these two problems in your own throwing or in your partner's, you should be able to correct it using that method.

The problem of moving prematurely for a trick catch can usually be corrected simply by calling it to the player's attention. If that's not enough, make the player wait until you yell "now!" before moving to make the catch (or have your partner yell for you if you're the one moving too soon).

For every student I've taught who threw too weakly, I've had sixty who tried to throw too hard. Just relax and throw with the least effort necessary to get the disc to your partner with good spin and a good, steady flight. In several types of deliveries, a flick of the wrist, even with the rest of the body held rigid, can send the disc sailing thirty meters. So take it easy. The best drill I know of for learning any new throw is Frisbee May I: you and your partner start out practicing the throw at a range of about five meters. When both of you are throwing consistently well, each of you may take a giant step back, and so on and on until you are thirty or forty meters apart. That way you learn quickly which movements of the hand are essential for propelling the disc, which movements impart spin, which movements assist as the range increases, and so forth.

Another bit of advice for beginners: don't overdo practice at first. For one thing, you can get a case of Frisbee finger—a raw spot caused by the abrasion of the disc on untoughened hands during repeated practice of a particular style of delivery. A severe case of Frisbee finger could cause you to have to skip a day of playing and might even require a band-aid. For another thing, evidence indicates that physical skills are learned most efficiently in a regular program of forty- to eighty-minute sessions, daily or every other day. Most players I've ever known, though, can't put a disc down until their arm is ready to go down with it. If you can't keep to a regular practice schedule, at least, remember that your first hour is your best. Do your playing to learn then and your playing to play afterward.

If your experience with the disc is fairly limited, let me suggest some throws and catches to learn before you try to cope with the details of spin, flight, trick variations, and so on. Throws: learn level flights and skips for the backhand, the sidearm and/or the thumber, and the overhand wrist flip. Learn the roll curve, skip curve, and hover with a backhand. Try the upside-down wrist flip. Catches: learn bth, btb, and btl catches and the cross-body trail, all with both right and left hands. Practice the set-up, a few tips, and the finger-spinning catch. When you get to the point that you are accurate with all those throws four times out of five at a range of twenty-five meters or so, and when you can consistently make four out of five of each of the catches, you can go ahead and figure that you're at the intermediate level.

INTERMEDIATE PRACTICE

There is a hazy distinction between beginning and intermediate practice. Basically, the objective of beginning practice is diversification—learning a variety of techniques. The purpose of intermediate practice tends more toward generalization—learning to do each of the techniques in a variety of ways and under a variety of conditions. Some reasons a technique can vary: use of different discs, different wind conditions, the demands of the various games, different playing partners and playing areas, variation in the muscles in use immediately prior to execution of the technique, and so on. No technique is learned until it is overlearned, until you've had such extensive experience with it that you can execute it automatically in a wide variety of playing conditions.

There is also a hazy distinction between the beginning and the intermediate player. The intermediate player might be characterized as having developed a well enough integrated skill background for verbal instruction to become meaningful. Building a vocabulary to cover learned skills helps the intermediate player to analyze her or his own play, it makes retention of skills easier, and it allows players to discuss their skills—to exchange pointers, in other words.

Always, understanding and a skill vocabulary lag behind performance. I urge you, therefore, to play first and read second, play again, read again. Cover only a few skills at a time, go out and practice, then come back and read in a little more detail.

To emphasize the point futher, people learn new skills just as fast or faster after a brief demonstration, followed by trial-and-error practice without any verbal instruction, than they do with even simple, brief instructions. That has been shown experimentally many times. I mentioned three cases where I would step in to instruct a student, but those cases involve violation of the essential mechanical principles of the skill. When the problem is one of degree—too little spin, too much arm in the throw, lack of versatility in a particular style of delivery, and so forth—I find the easiest way to correct it is simply to pair the student up with another who performs the skill in question well. If I return after a few minutes to find the problem is not remedying itself, I can always expect to hear a bunch of self-analytical comments and questions ("I think I need to get my shoulder more forward. Do you think I'm releasing too early?") that often aren't related to Frisbee skills at all, much less to the problem I was concerned with in the first place.

Switching off your conscious mind is not so easy, and it's not exactly what you're after anyway. You want to learn to communicate back and forth between the two levels of your mind. At first, that involves a sort of "forgetting out" of the conscious mind to give the skill-learning mind a head start. Just stay fascinated by the flight of the disc, get into the flow of freestyle, and don't be concerned about performance.

As skills approach advanced levels, it is useful to break practice up into four parts: part drill, rehearsal, mental rehearsal, and galumphing. Part drill is the exploration of subtle changes in a maneuver. You correct or alter a small part and reinsert it into the whole movement. Rehearsal means practice toward getting skills down pat. For instance, you and your partner might work out a freestyle routine, then rehearse it until it is faultless and automatic. Another example would be working on a drill with your ultimate team until it starts to click.

Mental rehearsal involves picturing your playing skills in your mind, whether you are analyzing for improvements, seeking new variations, or just visualizing a set of skills prior to their performance. Mental rehearsal implies that the ability to communicate between conscious mind and skill-learning mind has been achieved. Galumphing is playing for the merriment of it. Not only do you do it because Frisbee is essentially a fun sport, but also because it is a time when a lot of new moves will come to you spontaneously. More about that in chapter 1.

1. Frisbee

Is there still daylight out? Then skip over to chapter 2 and skim through it until you find a couple of throws you'd like to try. Get out your favorite Frisbee disc and go get your favorite Frisbee partner. Come back and read this chapter tonight. One other thing: catching is half of Frisbee. While your partner's getting ready, skim through chapter 10 to see what catches you'd like to try.

FRISBEE: PAST, PRESENT, AND FUTURE

Two gentlemen, Fred Morrison and Warren Francioni, handcrafted the first plastic flying disc in 1948. They put the design into production soon after, and, with that, the first honest-to-gosh flying disc was born. (Pie pans, can lids, and whatnot had been sailed now and then in earlier years.) Wham-O Manufacturing Company of San Gabriel, California, bought the idea from Morrison in 1955 and began production of their own flying disc in 1957. In 1959 Wham-O trademarked the name "Frisbee."

In its first decade the flying disc evolved from a novelty sold at county fairs to a toy sold in stores throughout the United States. With the production of the Pro Model Frisbee in 1964, flying discs evolved from toy to sporting good. By that time millions of people were playing Frisbee, and each year after that saw millions more play Frisbee for the first time.*

The '70s have seen a dramatic increase in public enthusiasm, media interest, organizations and tournaments, and people who play with the Frisbee disc as their primary recreational activity. Two million people saw Victor Malafronte and John Kirkland do their hot Frisbee routine when they toured with the Harlem Globetrotters in 1974. By now millions more have seen state-of-the-art Frisbee demonstrations at professional and college basketball, football, and soccer games from Boston to San Francisco. Frisbee play has cracked such sports bastions as *ABC's Wide World of Sports*, *CBS Sports Spectacular*, and *Sports Illustrated*. But perhaps the best indication that the disc has arrived is the way scenes of frolicking picnickers and beachgoers sailing their brightly colored saucers have started to crop up in advertisements for everything from beer to Bermuda—wherever the advertiser

Frisbee by Stancil Johnson offers a much more complete history of Frisbee. It also contains outstanding information on Frisbee games, the different varieties of discs, and many other facets of Frisbee not covered extensively in this book.

wants the product quickly associated with leisure time.

The '80s will see millions of people take up Frisbee as their primary athletic interest. There will be Frisbee stadiums, league play at every level from grade school to professional, and regularly scheduled, nationally televised tournaments.

FRISBEE: WHAT IT IS, WHAT IT IS

A sign that Frisbee play is deepening its impression on the public mind is the increasing frequency with which it is referred to as a sport. But Frisbee is not, speaking technically for a moment, a sport.

For years the Frisbee disc carried an inscription on its underside that began, "Play catch, invent games." About thirty or forty million people have played catch with a saucer. But catch is not a sport. It's not even a game. It's a pastime.*

One of the joys of Frisbee is that it *is* a pastime—free and unstructured, uncomplicated by rules.

Most other popular recreational activities are also merely pastimes—ice skating, jogging, swimming, hang gliding, skateboarding, and hundreds of others. But there is a difference. Most pastimes are basically individual activities. Catch, on the other hand, is, like chase, a collaborative activity; it doesn't exist unless at least two people are doing it. Such two-party pastimes lend themselves so readily to games that they usually almost cease to exist as pastimes. The earliest recreational activities were collaborative, and our major games and sports began as collaborative pastimes. Football and baseball, for instance, can trace their roots back to the prehistoric (and preadolescent) recreation of chunking clods and gourds.*

To get back to the second half of the inscription, dozens, maybe even hundreds, of games have been invented to be played with a flying disc. I wouldn't want to try to guess how many thousand people have invented games for Frisbee (some of the games are so basic that they are certain to have been invented many times), but I would guess that

*Brian Sutton-Smith had this to say about pastimes in a paper he presented to the American Anthropological Association: "Pastimes do not have winners and they may not have aides. Yet like games, they are voluntary activities with their own particular rules, and they do have uncertainty with respect to outcomes. Instead of players contesting with each other, however, they combine together to act out a contest between the forces of order and disorder. I like to think that these games illustrate the basic issue in all co-operation, which is whether the playing group can maintain its existence against the normally divisive forces which

play upon it. While it has often been pointed out that competition implies co-operation because the players must be able to agree about the rules, it has not been generally realized, that there are games whose major focus had been the question of that co-operation; games whose focus is the antithesis between order and disorder." Disorder in Frisbee is bad throws and missed catches.

*Stancil Johnson wrote a very enlightening and humorous article on the origins of ball sports and disc sports that appeared in the September 1976 *Smithsonian*.

about half the people who have ever tossed a Frisbee disc have tried one or more of the games from basebee to netbee. The four Frisbee games described in the introduction—guts, ultimate, golf, and freestyle—have become sports in their own right, that is, they have acquired the trappings of sports—league play, standing teams, professional associations, and spectator interest. So Frisbee play is not a sport. It is four sports (with more on the way). It is also a hundred or so games, the field-meet contests, several tricks and stunts, and at its heart it is a pastime.

It used to be that if you said, "Let's play Frisbee," everyone knew what you meant. Now you have to be more specific: "Let's head out to the ultimate field," or "Let's round up some guts players," or, "Let's freestyle."

You might have wondered, incidentally, from what I said about collaborative pastimes turning rapidly into games and sports whether Frisbee is doomed to exist soon only in the competitive realm. Actually, the fact that freestyle has become a sport without significant change in its format is the very indication that it won't. Freestyle is the first pure catch game interesting enough to be a sport in its own right (in tournaments, it is a game and a sport by virtue of a judges' scoring system.) It's not going to end up as solely a backyard, Sunday-afternoon enterprise, and it's not going to end up as just another ulcer sport. It'll be everything in between.

As you can see, Frisbee has gone through a lot of changes recently, more than even most avid players (discophiles, as we call ourselves) can keep up with. This book will have its hands full just trying to cover the advances in freestyle of the last three or four years. If you want to know more about the many other facets of Frisbee, you'll have to wait for the next book someone writes, or else write the International Frisbee Association.

THE APPLE BLOSSOM THEORY

Even though the sport is still young after thirty years (it's not very far along as sports evolution goes), its development has obviously been speeded up by its position on the family tree of throwing and catching games. Up to this point, Frisbee games have been devised largely by simple substitution of a disc for a ball. Of course, the character of the game changes; just as it would if a brick of anything else had been the replacement, but usually with a Frisbee lively new dimensions are added to the strategy. (Notice, however, that a Frisbee disc does not work out very well in racket-type games.)

Frisbee play is not all imitation. What does make it different from all other forms of catch is that a saucer flies. However, until three or four years ago, no players were making significant use of that fact. Sure, from the very beginning the curving, soaring flights of discs gave them their appeal and set them apart from the mere arching trajectories of balls. The realization that you could throw a disc in one direction and have it arrive accurately at a target that lay in another direction came early, as did the discovery that a disc can be made to skip (not bounce) off a hard surface. Later, the disc was found to fly as well upside-down as rightside-up. These were all discoveries about the flight properties of the Frisbee disc. Still, however, the game was being played with a set of mental attitudes that had not really opened to the potentials of flight. The difference at that point between playing catch with a ball and playing it with a disc did not lie in the essentials of throwing and catching but simply in how the thing that was thrown traveled between throw and catch.

Finally, about 1973, the air bounce began to catch on. The air bounce is a way of throwing a disc, using any of several different styles of delivery, so that the disc springs up off a cushion of air that piles up on its underside during flight (see chapter 8). Coincidentally, this was taking place about the time Stancil Johnson was completing work on *Frisbee: A Practitioner's Manual and Definitive Treatise*. Dr. Johnson mentions the air bounce briefly in his book, calling it a "dip" and listing it under the heading "Flight Peculiarities." Peculiar or not, the air bounce had a spectacular impact on Frisbee. It demonstrated that the manner of release, not just the angle of release, could influence the flight of the disc. It followed that if the disc's flight can be manipulated during the throw the same was probably true for the catch, and so it is.

Actually, the leap of the imagination that was necessary was not to any new way of catching (conceivably, any way you can catch a Frisbee, you can also catch a ball) but to controlling the flight of the disc without catching it. By the early '70s, many players were using tips, thumping the disc on the underside as it passed (see chapter 13). The first tips were rather crude, more like setting up a volleyball than a saucer, but by 1975 tips were being used to change the angle and direction of the disc's flight in numerous subtle ways. Tipping and the air bounce gave players a new way of looking at the sport—they removed the blinders, so to speak. New realms of play opened up, and a torrent of new playing techniques followed. This new consciousness has started filtering out into every facet of play. Even distance throwing has become as much a matter of playing the disc on the wind as of raw throwing power.

Of course, too, there are a lot of things you can do with a disc that you can't do with a ball simply because balls lack rims and large flat surfaces. (On the other hand, a Frisbee does not dribble as well as a basketball.) Flight alone does not account for the success of Frisbee. Boomerangs and balsawood gliders fly, but they are not particularly well suited to games of catch. As it turns out, the features of a Frisbee make it not only adequate as a throwing object, but superior. By the same token, if Frisbee discs were only ingenious throwing objects incapable of flight, freestyle with a Frisbee would differ from freestyle with a ball, as in the Harlem Globetrotters' performance with a basketball in their *Sweet Georgia Brown* routine, only in terms of the number of techniques possible with each, not in terms of the essence of the action.

The marriage of flight and advanced throwing design is the basis for my Apple Blossom Theory, which holds that Frisbee was never a branch on the family tree of throwing and catching games, but a flower. The flower was cross-pollinated. The fruit developed and dropped from the tree. When the seedling, a hybrid of catch and flight, sprouted about four years ago, the sport came into its own. I made some bold predictions earlier about what the sport would be like in the next decade. This theory is part of the support for those claims. Frisbee is a sapling that will grow to be a great tree. Who knows yet whether it will be a tall, fast-growing pine that several thousand players will ride to heights of perfection; a broad, sturdy oak whose limbs will reach out to millions; or a giant sequoia that will dominate the forest of sports and recreation.

KEEPING UP WITH FRISBEE

I hope what I have said so far hasn't given you the impression that the game has changed and left you behind. There are many more discophiles who haven't heard of such things as upside-down throws and air bounces than there are those who have. New techniques are being added to Frisbee at such an incredible rate that unless you go to half a dozen tournaments a year, subscribe to *Frisbee World*, and correspond with players in all parts of the country you could not hope to keep up.

The sport is developing, and past a certain point in its development it came into its own. But that doesn't mean there is a whole new style you have to learn in order to be considered a Frisbee player. If you play with a disc, you're a Frisbee player.

The first and only rule of disc sports still is, "Play it your way." This book is not a guide to what you need to know to become a complete, all-around Frisbee player; it is a guide to your own imagination. Select those throws and catches that interest you and fit them into your own style. If you're imaginative and willing to experiment, your style will develop on its own. But the best thing for anybody's style is exposure to a wide array of talented players and to their styles. There are, in fact, numerous regional and individual styles of play. Some styles emphasize speedy throws, others, stateliness or fluidity; some emphasize catching variety, others, throwing variety or both; some are played close in, some far apart, and so on. The one quality that characterizes all good styles is adaptability. Let your style be anything you want it to be except a rut.

Keeping up with the sport is increasingly a matter of communications. Make plans to participate in (or at least attend) a tournament in your area this year. But if your interest in Frisbee carries you no further than underhand throws and two-handed catches, you're still a Frisbee player and you can still have a lot of fun tossing the flying saucer.

THE REDEEMING SOCIAL VALUE THEORY

The purpose of providing you with another of my theories is not so much to offer further evidence of the important role the disc will soon have in sports and recreation but to show you what virtues Frisbee has to offer to sport.

Major sports are coming under increasing attack lately from critics within and without. There's probably not a coach in the country who hasn't had to defend the program against bitter assault over too much or too little emphasis on winning or competition or chauvinism. Actually, there is nothing at all wrong with any of our sports—maybe a bad incident here and there, but nothing basically wrong—except that many have run their course.*

Grumblings about change don't usually precede change: they precede junking. (Just think back to the last time someone you know talked about overhauling their car. Unless that person was a died-in-the-wool tinkerer, the chances are that your friend ended up getting a new car instead.)

If that's true, we'll soon see the dinosaur sports start doing their disappearing act to be replaced by new sports better suited to our needs. An examination of the current furor should reveal a great deal about where sports are headed. If you can get through all the steam that has been generated, you'll find three main issues doing the boiling: competition, creativity, and sex discrimination.

The most divisive issue at the moment seems to be competition: How can we keep putting all this unhealthy emphasis on competition over co-operation in an increasingly crowded and complex world *vs* How can you expect people to make their way through the harsh realities of life if they haven't been taught to compete. A clear way through that issue is provided by some recent psychological research. In a survey that measured the impact scientists have on their fields, the finding

*I don't mean to imply that all the criticism lacks substance. Clear voices always rise above the roar. In this case, I have found the following voices worth listening to: *The Ultimate Athlete* by George Leonard, *Golf in the Kingdom* by Michael Murphy, *The Inner Game of Tennis* by Timothy Gallwey, *Sports in America* by James A. Michener, and *Beyond Jogging* by Mike Spino. These books don't complain about sports; they offer new ways of perceiving sports and play. As such, they have sent a bigger ripple through the sports world than all the frontal attacks on sports combined.

was that, when other factors were even, scientists who measured low in competition contributed twice as much to their field as highly competitive scientists. For the highly competitive, competition seems to become an end in itself, and so it interferes when it comes to selecting appropriate ways to handle any of life's demands.

People who were not particularly competitive, interestingly, measured out higher in self-esteem, particularly when they were also competent, eager workers with a high desire to master skills. Looks bad for competition, except that this latter group was found to be perfectly capable of handling competition, even of enjoying it, but, most important, of being able to use it when it was called for.

What that suggests is that an ideal sport should first require the building of skills and should then be flexible enough to provide ways to apply those skills both collaboratively and competitively. Monika Lou, Women's World Frisbee Champion and three-time Women's Distance Champion (titles she went through stiff competition to win), wrote to me about the collaborative side: "Frisbee is a co-operative game; you're working *with* someone, not against anyone. It's like saying, 'Hey, look at us!' not, 'Look at me!' It's helping the other person to look good and enjoying yourself at the same time."

At the other end of the Frisbee spectrum is the game that goes beyond competition to unbridled (though harmless) aggression—guts. Ultimate teaches team co-operation. Golf teaches self-development. The field events teach co-operation with the elements. Freestyle teaches collaboration. Some other games involve one-against-one competition. Your ticket to all these games is a Frisbee disc that costs less than three dollars and a few basic throwing and catching skills. Name another sport that comes close to offering that variety.

The second issue, creativity, hasn't been quite so heated as the first, but is is probably a more important issue nevertheless. The concern is that success in too many sports is a matter of redundant, overly specialized movements and of following rules and orders with no room for creativity of the body or mind. Brian Sutton-Smith, who has made unparallelled contributions to the understanding of play and games, expresses the crucial importance of this issue in his forthcoming book, *A History of Children's Play*: "We might say that if the organization of sports in the first fifty years of this century was focussed amongst other things upon domestication of violence, the organization of play in the next fifty years may well be focussed upon the development of the capacity for imaginative innovation. Perhaps if a world civilization such as ours is to survive it can do so only by producing infinitely more people with such capacities."

The point was also made somewhat irreverently when someone mused recently that our heads of state could not hold their own in complex policy negotiations with the leaders of other nations because our leaders were weaned on football while the foreign leaders had cut their teeth on the more intricate games of chess, soccer, and go.

Freestyle (and Frisbee in general) is nothing if not creative motion and the invention of new techniques. As for innovation, if for no other reason than the historical accident of its recent origins, Frisbee is ripe for the invention of games and new strategies. Anyone who wants to devote a little time and thought could come up with a new Frisbee game and even stand a fair chance of seeing it become a national sport in a few years, as was the case with the Columbia High School students who invented ultimate.

Sex discrimination is the third hot spot, and there is every reason to be concerned about sports that by their nature exclude equal participation by half the population. There was even some worry about Frisbee games on this point, but I'm pleased to report that male Frisbee players have shown increasing improvement in grace, rhythm, balance, fluidity of motion, and self-expressiveness, and there is no longer any reason to suppose that men will not be able to play on an equal footing with women.

That may sound backwards, but my experience with my classes has been that women frequently pick up freestyle faster than men because they don't have to go through a period of adjusting to the use of finesse rather than force. Men are judged in too many sports merely by their home run hitting, the power of their punches, or their bone-jarring blocking. There's rough and tumble in Frisbee games, for sure, but there is also a large measure of subtle skills. Frisbee play offers athletes a chance for more total and complete self-expression. And women athletes who are looking around for a sport that offers lifelong enjoyment and in which the differences of gender disappear would do well to consider Frisbee.

One other of the many "socially redeeming values" of disc sports deserves at least brief mention, and that is, of course, the variety of benefits they can offer to school physical education programs. The disc has been finding its way into school, college, and park programs for years now, but in the last couple of years that trend has skyrocketed. Consider why:

- Incomparably low cost. One disc (retail value less than $3.00) can keep one to fourteen or more players happily occupied.

- Extremely low injury risk. So far, there are no Frisbee contact sports, and a disc, at four ounces, is all but incapable of causing as much as a bruise, even in guts.

- Flexibility. The basic skills of Frisbee play lend themselves to an incredible variety of games and contests which can be adapted to any number of players and any sort of playing area or conditions. Further, Frisbee provides an inexhaustible source of challenge and fun, whether used only as an occasional class activity or as a year-round program from the primary grades through high school and college (and as a lifetime sport after that on past retirement years).

Do I even need to mention the popularity of Frisbee play with students? And time after time it succeeds in attracting students who were previously uninterested in sports. Thirteen- and fifteen-year-olds learn faster than you can teach them. If it's your job to teach Frisbee to students in that approximate age range, just give them a fresh idea to work on every so often, then stand back and watch the creative juices flow. You can learn a lot yourself by watching them. Invariably, with a young teenager, I can teach most of the different deliveries and catches in an afternoon. (On the other hand, I was unable in two hours once to get a single successful overhand wrist flip from even one of a group of varsity athletes from a national championship football team.)

By now there are scores of players across the country who have taught Frisbee courses. If you would like to see Frisbee games in your school's athletic program, the International Frisbee Association can provide you with detailed information on setting up a successful program, and it can put you in touch with players in your area qualified to teach a regular course, to put on demonstrations or set up a tournament at the school, or to run a workshop on Frisbee skills for the school's own physical education instructors.

FLYING

People engage in sports seeking a sense of accomplishment and the sensation of living life vigorously. Reaching these goals produces confidence and exhilaration, the two greatest rewards sports can offer.

The potential of Frisbee to instill confidence should be obvious from what I have already said about women often learning faster than men and thirteen-year-olds learning faster than championship college athletes. The skills of Frisbee are different enough from other sports skills that everybody starts pretty much from scratch, and they are so very diverse that everybody usually gets several turns to "go to the head of the class."

A girl in one of my classes had done dismally on backhands, overhands, and thumbers. After three and a half class meetings, she was more than a little disheartened, and we were just getting ready to start on the sidearm, a throw that normally takes more practice and patience than any other. Her first sidearm was a beauty. Her third sidearm was a between-the-legs throw! And her fourth was a between-the-legs hike! She was jubilant. No one matched her sidearms all day.

That happens all the time in Frisbee classes, though usually not to such stark extremes. Some players have to work hard on techniques that come quickly to others, and then they find some techniques a snap that others find difficult. But the techniques that give the most difficulty are ultimately the most satisfying, because always the triumphant moment comes when the catch is finally made or when the throw at last falls into place.

As you will see in this book, there are enough Frisbee techniques to be mastered to keep anyone busy for a long time. But there is more to learning Frisbee than stringing a bunch of tricks together. Each technique you learn influences the skills you already have and will influence new skills as you learn them. The process is organic—each part is nourished by the others.

At the beginning of this book there was a quotation from Richard Fariña: "We find, upon climbing past the higher branches, that we all can fly." That is a perfect characterization of the way the skills of Frisbee are learned. You make your way up the trunk with the skills you bring to the sport (and I've seen players with backgrounds in everything from ballet to martial arts—if you have other talents, express them in your Frisbee play). The branches are the different throwing and catching techniques. At first, you move back to the trunk before trying to reach up to the next branch. Once you've tested the branches, though, you can climb from branch to branch and make your way further and further out along each branch each time you come back to it.

Soon, when you're fairly familiar with the tree and you're climbing with ease, something else takes place. You lose yourself for a moment in a game of freestyle and you suddenly find that you have just done some amazing feat—something you have never practiced, maybe never even thought of. But it felt perfectly natural. Or suddenly you get the sensation that you, your partner, and the disc are flawlessly tied into a sort of universal rhythm and everything seems to flow with extreme ease. That's flying. You are no longer climbing among the branches, but moving freely.

What I call flying is not something I made up. It is a sensation known to many athletes and trainers. It is exhilaration, but it is more than just the exhilaration of a good workout—it is peak exhilaration. You can only fly when your body and mind are in harmony—when you are physically and mentally absorbed in what you are doing. When you work hard at something and find it stimulating and motivating, it stays with you even when you set it aside for a while. Your subconscious mind makes connections that never occurred to your conscious mind. When you go back to play, your subconscious mind pipes in and a new move is born or your play becomes so vivid and crisp that it seems perfect.

Flying comes most readily when creativity, spontaneity, and flowing action are the ingredients of the game.* As I've already said, we are overbur-

*Risk sports, such as hang gliding, sky diving, and deep-sea diving, are particularly noted for promoting peak experiences. Frisbee is not widely considered a risk sport, though an occasional picnicker or pedestrian will complain of the

dened with sports that require specialized, repetitious, monotonous movements swing after swing, play after play, inning after inning—circumstances not conducive to flying. How often could you hope to achieve peak exhilaration as a fielder in a baseball game? Prolonged periods of spontaneous creativity are common in the thick of freestyle. It's a rare Frisbee player who doesn't have a multitude of peak experiences to recount.

FRISBEE: THE GREAT COMMUNICATOR

The only goal of freestyle is to keep the disc flowing between two or more people. The only skills necessary to do that are the ability to throw a good, catchable throw (one that's neither slow and wobbly nor streaking like a bullet and that doesn't always curve off course) and to make some sort of catch and get off a return throw without undue delay. Anyone can learn those skills in at most a day or two, usually in a few minutes. After that, they can invite themselves into any Frisbee game, no

risk of being hit with your Frisbee. Do be considerate of others when you play. I did have one friend years back who managed to turn Frisbee into a risk sport. He used a black Master to bean the large and ill-humored bully of the school —simply for the sport of it. However, he miscalculated the advantage the distance of the throw would give him for making his escape, and he ended up having the exact opposite of a peak experience.

matter if the other players are World Class Masters, without fear that they will detract from the game.

I play regularly with some excellent players who are less than half my age and with one woman who is double my age, who has some dynamite throws. I've also had some splendid games with players who had only a few minutes of playing experience and command of only one type of throw. On the one hand, even the fanciest freestyle tricks can be learned at almost any age. On the other hand, even great difference in playing proficiency between two players matters little to the success and enjoyment of the game.

Frisbee has been exported in recent years to England, Germany, France, Australia, Japan, and other countries, and is getting enthusiastic receptions. I have taken a saucer to parks in several countries and found myself instantly surrounded by dozens of curious, eager players. I have had terrific games with players who couldn't understand a word I said, and countless Peace Corps volunteers, tourists, and soldiers stationed overseas can also tell you how much they relied on the language of the disc.

A Frisbee disc is always irresistible. One flight of the disc soars over barriers of age, culture, language, and class. In fact, I imagine that the simple question, "Do you mind if I play?" has been responsible for more friendships in the last thirty years than any other.

2. Backhand Family

Backhands offer control, accuracy, and versatility. You can put any amount of spin on the disc, throw with a quick stroke, a slow stroke, an accelerating stroke, a long stroke, or a short stroke. You can throw with your arm held close in or extended at full length. You can start breaking your wrist at the beginning of the stroke or you can postpone it until right before release to get more snap into the spin. There are more variations in backhand grips than could possibly be described. The backhand works superbly for every type of flight, but particularly hovers, skips, and rollers.

A straight and level backhand.

The classic backhand grip.

The Berkeley grip.

42

In fact, backhands delivered at angles between skip hyzer and roll hyzer probably account for more than fifty percent of all throws, even at advanced levels of play. However, there was a time not so long ago when the backhand, along with its cousin the underhand, accounted for virtually one hundred percent of all throws.

Delivery angles for the backhand family. Closed stance:
(a) multiple skip, (b) underhand pull, (c) skip, (d) level
flight, (e) roll curve, (f) roller, (g) upside-down. Open
stance: (h) upside-down, (i)
water skip, (j) underhand,
(k) underhand skip, (l) behind the back.

At first, learn a level backhand using a moderate
stroke and a good snap of the wrist. Get your delivery grooved so that you can reproduce it time and
again as nearly the same as possible. As you get
your backhand grooved, experiment with the speed
of the flight. Then try varying the spin. Feeders are
throws that get to the catcher with a lot of spin
but little forward momentum. When you and your
partner can consistently exchange nice, steady,
level feeders, catching practice becomes a breeze.

Everyone who has played with a disc is probably
familiar with the classic backhand grip. It's a fan
grip with the forefinger stretched out along the lip.
A modified fist grip, commonly known as the
Berkeley grip, is gaining favor, and it does offer
mechanical advantages. The forefinger hooks snugly around the edge of the rim (some variations find
the forefinger around the edge to a greater or lesser

degree) and can impart more spin and distance to the throw with the same effort in the delivery than the classic backhand grip is able to.

There is little question that the Berkeley grip is superior, and I recommend it, though it feels more awkward at first. There are, however, plenty of variations of the backhand grip in between the fist grip (Berkeley power grip) and the classic grip. The thumb can move anywhere from the flight rings to the lip. The forefinger can move all over the rim.

A backhand can be flipped from just about any position to set up brushing and other discwork techniques.

The delivery of a roller. At the angle the disc was released, it will veer back to the thrower's left on landing.

And the other three fingers can move from all firm against the cheek to any number scattered around on the underside of the flight plate.

Good sports sense would dictate that, after you find the grip for you, you adopt it by drilling on it over and over and then using it exclusively. However, continuous exploration, experimentation, and learning are part of what Frisbee is about. So, decide for yourself whether you are going to settle down with one grip or use a variety of them.

Lower the arm from the position for level delivery and try some curved and banked flights. With your arm in a lowered position, you will be throwing skip curves. To make the disc skip, simply throw a skip curve out away from you and, if it lands on a suitably hard surface, it will skip. In-variably, most people will try to skip the disc by nosing it into the ground three or four meters in front of them. That's the way I started, and that does seem an awfully logical way to do it. But it doesn't work. The physics of the matter require that the disc set down on its forward-spinning shoulder if it is to skip.

If you first learn to throw a good, long, low skip curve and then start lowering your sights until the disc begins hitting down about three-fourths of the way to your partner, you should learn skips without much trouble. Once you get a few successful skips, learning to vary them comes easily. Generally, the closer in and harder you throw the disc down, the higher it will rise after the skip. You can get multiple skips by landing the disc down more

A backhand throw in a game of ultimate.

The release position for a skip.

nearly vertical (see diagram of backhand delivery angles), and the curved path the disc follows as it skips around will widen out too. Make allowance for the curve as you aim.

Finally, when you land the disc down vertical or even past vertical, you'll get a gym-floor curve.

Keep the disc low on the delivery to minimize its tendency to rebound from the ground on impact. Backhand gym-floor curves yield wide "C"-shaped curves left-handed and "Ɔ"-shaped right-handed.

Raise the arm from the position for level delivery to get roll curves and banks. Getting the disc to roll is not at all difficult, but getting it to roll accurately can be tricky. The direction the disc will take off on a roller depends on the exact angle at which it strikes the ground and will vary somewhat from one type of surface to the next. Rollers are tremendously important in golf for getting around

A btb backhand is a fairly weak throw, but a three-arm throw, as shown here, can be thrown briskly. The arm builds up a good deal of momentum as it circles around the body. To anyone new to the disc, the three-arm is an eye-opening throw. Add a pivot at the end of the throw, and it becomes a trick almost impossible for anyone with an unpracticed eye to follow.

The release position for an upside-down backhand. Normally, the arm will continue down and across in the follow-through.

and under obstacles. I know of a hole on one disc golf course where the best shot to the "green" is a roller along a slanted wall.

Hover flights, as indicated in the introduction, are thrown to climb at a slight angle, then stall out and settle down to the catcher. Getting the disc to settle down in the right range without sliding off takes a well-practiced stroke and good spin. Hovers are very important for catching practice and especially important for discwork. If you and your partner want to excel at freestyle, hovers are indispensable.

A btb backhand is a fairly weak throw, because, with the back in the way, the throw is almost all wrist. Still, it is widely used in freestyle. Most often, it is seen in the form of a three-arm throw (commonly referred to as the phony btb throw), which is simply a btb backhand with a lot of window dressing added on the front end.

The name "three-arm" derives from the way the disc seems to be thrown first forward, then backward, then around behind the back. When first used in guts, it was a great demoralizer. The catching team would dive for the first fake and then lie in a pile to watch a gentle throw sail overhead. However, the time when a three-arm could deceive any but the greenest guts team has long passed. The backhand can be thrown between the legs as well as behind the back, and you can even get a sort of three-arm btl throw.

An upside-down backhand is thrown simply by

unleashing the disc from a coiled position over the shoulder. The throw is called a Sal shot in some quarters, but the name has never caught on widely. The stroke is easily reproducible because the arm is laid over as far as it will go, making it easy to find the groove every time. However, it seems to be necessary in the stroke to follow through down and across the intended direction of flight and to turn the shoulder well down too. If you have a supple arm, you can make the throw with a long, lassoey windup.

On into the third decade of disc sports a fierce argument raged about which was the more powerful throw—the backhand or the underhand. Well, it has since been shown that neither is the most powerful throw. The backhand, at least, is powerful, and it has many other virtues besides, as you have seen. The underhand, however, is a relatively weak

Ed Headrick's Disc Pole Hole has revolutionized disc golf. Ed is shown here putting backhanded using a Fastback Frisbee.

The backhand push is one of those rare throws that gets left spin when thrown from the right side of the body. That matters little, since getting much spin at all is difficult. In freestyle, a push can be masked by all sorts of pivots and other body movements.

throw without much versatility. It works well for skips and skip curves, but, as you begin to approach the angle for level delivery, what power and control the throw does offer fade fast. This once prevalent delivery is pretty rare these days.

A water skip is what comes of an overhand delivery with a backhand grip. The push is the throw you get with a forehanded delivery and a classic

An underhand delivery shown here as normally made—in an open stance taking a step forward, almost like bowling.

A backhand feeder being readied. The tail is raised and will slap down (beavertail) somewhat during the stroke to help float the flight (see chapter 8). Also, notice the flying disc ring on the middle finger of the cuffing hand (see chapter 14).

backhand grip. The disc is held by the tail rightside-up. (Upside-down pushes are interesting but not very useful.) Focus on getting a smoothly accelerating stroke and on rolling the disc off the forefinger or middle finger. It's a throw that can't take much force and so won't go very far—twenty meters top range. Still, it is very handy for its quick release in both close-range freestyle and ultimate.

A name you might want to be familiar with, though it is not yet widely used, is "pull." A pull is a backhand throw delivered from between the legs or underhanded in a closed stance—any position in which the throwing arm is strained and the disc can at best be gripped only by the nose. If a toss gripped by the tail is a push, then one gripped by the nose obviously should be a pull.

3. Forehand Family

The term "forehand" does not mean much in Frisbee throws. A forehand made with the palm turned downward or backward would likely be referred to as an overhand throw, and a forehand with the palm turned upward or forward would be called a sidearm. But, in fact, the customary sports names for types of strokes—sidearm, backhand, underhand, and so forth—were applied early in the history of Frisbee to particular types of deliveries.

In a number of cases, the name for a stroke has grown to be more closely associated with a grip than the stroke. So, for instance, as you probably noted in the previous chapter, an upside-down

The two-finger sidearm grip. The thumb should press firmly between the two fingers on the underside of the disc.

The thumber grip. The two middle fingers are often used to press the disc against the forearm to keep the grip sturdy during the stroke.

backhand is not thrown with anything like a backhand stroke. Backhand there refers to the grip. If it did refer to the stroke, upside-down backhand would be the name for what is properly known as an overhand-wrist-flip barrel-roll curve.

That may sound confusing, but it's not really. Knowing the grip used and the flight produced will tell you the stroke, whereas, knowing the stroke and the flight won't always reveal the grip. So grip, as mentioned in the introduction, is the most important determinant in naming Frisbee throws. Just don't let the fact that some of the grip families carry names more commonly associated in sports with a stroke throw you (so to speak).

Still, the term "forehand" has not latched itself onto either a grip or a stroke in Frisbee terminology. I have elected to use the term, because, to save space, I am including thumbers along with the

The delivery angles for sidearm throws. Closed stance: (a) cross-body blind, (b) gym-floor curve, (c) the cut (a sort of sidearmed version of the underhand, or vice versa), (d) water skip, (e) cross-body upside-down, (f) upside down. Open stance: (g) upside-down, (h) roller, (i) roll curve, (j) level flight, (k) skip, (l) btb skip curve, (m) btb multiple skip.

discussion of sidearms, and "forehand" is the one heading that covers both.

On close analysis, the thumber grip (with the thumb along the cheek and the fingers pressing just below the flight rings) is pretty much the same thing to the wrist-flip grip that the fist grip is to the classic backhand grip. However, the close resemblance of the thumber and the wrist-flip carries over to delivery angles only for throws made from a closed stance. The delivery angles for thumbers in an open stance almost exactly duplicate those of sidearms. Since thumbers are much more commonly thrown from an open stance, it seems more logical to group them with sidearms, regardless of the argument that they are more closely related to the overhand wrist flip, which is discussed in the next chapter.

Like all grip families, the thumber and sidearm

offer numerous variations. The only major variation of the thumber is the one I call the greater thumber. The thumb pad and heel of the palm press against the underside of the flight plate, and only the palp of the thumb remains against the cheek.

The sidearm has several important grip variations, which will be discussed in detail. First, let me say that sidearms are temperamental throws. Because the disc is propelled by the very tip of the middle finger (usually), sidearms have the longest reach of any throw. Also, unless a special effort is made, sidearms are delivered with comparatively less spin than backhands and wrist flips. The combination of long reach and little spin makes the

The snap-thumber grip. A snap of the fingers sends the disc on its way.

sidearm somewhat less stable than most types of throws, and that in turn makes it a trickier throw to master than most. But once it is mastered, it is every bit as much an all-purpose throw as the backhand. There are a small but growing number of players who prefer the sidearm over the backhand in all aspects of play—even accuracy throwing.

And why not use a sidearm for accuracy? Though it is thrown from a position far from the line of vi-

The thumber throw.

sion and thus impossible to actually aim, its long reach allows it to make highly efficient use of arm motion. It is therefore a throw that can be easily grooved. Experienced sidearm throwers can count on an excellent degree of accuracy—more from feel than from aim.

Beginners are seldom aware of the tremendous efficiency of sidearms, and so they often throw with much more force than necessary to get the distance they seek. Not only can that be a problem, particularly when some of the force is provided by the wrong muscles, but the sidearm is one throw that really benefits from being learned starting with the most nearly effortless stroke possible and then adding force by degrees.

A good sidearm is forty percent finger, thirty percent wrist, twenty percent forearm, and ten per-

Maximum efficiency is obtained when the elbow is kept tucked in close to the side. An almost effortless stroke can send the disc flying twenty or thirty meters.

A btb sidearm can be hurled just about as far as a regular sidearm. However, the harder you throw, the more you want to make sure to keep your rear end out of the way.

cent upper arm and body. So, begin with the finger, and begin at a range of about ten meters. Throw with your elbow comfortably close to the hip, but fling those throws from the very tip of your finger. You should have no insurmountable problems in developing a good sidearm on your own in this way, though, goodness knows, the sidearm is prone to a rash of problems. Just remember, virtually every sidearm ailment can be cured by the use of less force rather than more force, so long as you keep that finger working crisply.

The differences in the sidearm grips are a result of the two possible motions of the wrist. You can wave up and down (bye-bye) or side to side (so-long). Twisting, or rolling, the wrist is actually a motion of the forearm. The classic two-fingered sidearm uses the so-long motion with the hand in a supinated (palm-up) position. Basically, the only

The cross-body blind sidearm is used extensively in freestyle. Often the throw is made with the body pivoting in the direction opposite that of the stroke.

In a thumber, as the forearm is angled up, the hand can be angled down to maintain the hyzer for a level flight, much more so than is possible with a sidearm.

A sidearm delivery. The large backswing and the full arm movement indicate that the throw is probably intended to go fifty meters or more.

thus perhaps produces more spin and, consequently, more flight stability. I was surprised when it dawned on me how many of the players whose sidearms I really admire use the one-fingered sidearm. I still use the standard two-finger grip, but I think more and more about changing.

The one-finger grip is launched with the forefinger against the cheek. The middle finger (in the bye-bye, not the so-long) is braced against the edge or sometimes does not even touch the disc. I call the two-finger bye-bye sidearm a flick grip. The middle finger goes against the cheek, and the index and middle fingers are held nearly perpendicular to each other, so that the index finger points to about the center of the disc. The disc cannot be cocked as far back with this grip, and a good deal of the

variations of the classic sidearm follow from the number of fingers (one to four) placed under the disc. The standard two fingers are far and away better than any other combinations.

The other important sidearm variations employ the bye-bye motion, and here the one-fingered sidearm is the most important version. The bye-bye motion is whippier than the so-long motion and

Good sidearm rollers are an invaluable asset to any player's golf game. The jarring effects of landing impact are decreased the closer the disc is released to the ground.

tension in the grip is nonproductive. Still, the grip embraces a good amount of surface area and so is very sturdy.

The Texas twister is a hermaphrodite grip—half thumber, half sidearm. You can consider it either a thumber with the forefinger brought under and laid along the cheek or a one-fingered sidearm with the thumb brought under and laid along the cheek. It's only a novelty grip.

The thumber, and especially, the sidearm can be thrown in any position possible with any other grip, and then some. The btb sidearm (or thumber), unlike the btb backhand, is a power throw. Distances in the eighty-meter range have often been obtained with the btb sidearm. There's no problem getting level flight at long range; turnover will level the disc. In fact, I have often found it helpful to teach a btb sidearm to students who can't get the hang of hyzer in the regular sidearm. If you don't put enough hyzer on a btb throw, you'll smack yourself in the butt (what Johnson calls "the thwart of Thor"). Getting level flights at moderate range presents the same sort of problem that the underhand presents—difficulty maintaining control and versatility. When a btb sidearm gets used in freestyle, it gets used mostly for its skips, multiple skips, and gym-floor curves.

Sidearms offer a variety of blind throws: crossbody, btl hike, and onside. You have to stretch some to get a cross-body blind throw with a thumb-

A sidearm skip thrown between the legs. Skips are easy with btl throws, but to get a level flight the back must be arched considerably.

er. Several forward btl throws are possible with both sidearm and thumber.

The accuracy of upside-down sidearms and thumbers astonishes many people. The upside-down thumber, by the way, carries the name "dream shot" because the idea for the throw came to its originator, John Weyand, in a dream (a case of night flying). The accuracy is not so astonishing when you think about the fact that they are delivered more nearly along the line of vision than any other throw. Many players who have put on demonstrations in basketball courts have been able to put more than half their shots through the basket using an upside-down sidearm or thumber when throwing from the foul line in the far half of the court!

The upside-down throws start out with a looping curve to the offside, which adds to the astonishment at their accuracy, but which makes them a little less accurate at close range before the curve straightens out. All upside-down throws begin doing weird things after about forty meters at the most; so, really, the sidearm upside-down throw is only exceptionally accurate at moderate range. Upside-down throws, I should mention, are very seldom allowed in guts games. That's just as well, because use of the dream shot really overloads the game in favor of the throwing side.

The cocked position for an upside-down sidearm.

Just to show that a sidearm can be delivered from virtually any imaginable position: Jo Cahow's inverted btl hike.

4. Overhand Family

First, let me say that the names "overhand wrist flip," "overhand throw," and "wrist-flip" are interchangeable. Then, let me say that, whatever you call the overhand wrist flip, the throw itself is the essence of grace. It can be delivered with a long, lazy loop of the arm or with a swift, snappy release. Some players throw the wrist flip with very fluid motion, others with elastic movements. No matter what style of play the wrist flip is adapted to, it remains a very attractive throw.

Unlike the backhand, sidearm, and thumber, which are best thrown with conservative arm movements, the wrist flip uses liberal arm movement. But I don't want to give the impression that it is *thrown* with a great deal of arm. Any overhand delivery suffers the serious mechanical disadvantage of the elbow being locked out of the action, which is why the wrist flip can't compete with the backhand and sidearm for distance, despite the fact that it offers long reach and full body rotation.

A flip of the wrist is not nearly as powerful with the elbow turned behind the wrist as it is with the elbow ahead of the wrist, where it can provide leverage. This disadvantage is compensated for by the flow of the arm that leads up to the flip of the wrist at release. Very little force of the arm is required to get the flow.

The only important variation in the wrist-flip grip involves whether the middle finger goes back on the flight plate, as is customary, or moves down alongside the forefinger against the lip, shifting the stability of the grip toward the leading edge. In either case, the fingers on the flight plate should exert enough downward pressure to lock the edge of the disc on the top of the forearm—a very important point!

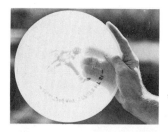

The wrist-flip grip.

The wrist-flip grip locked on the forearm in the cocked position. This variation uses two fingers on the lip.

58

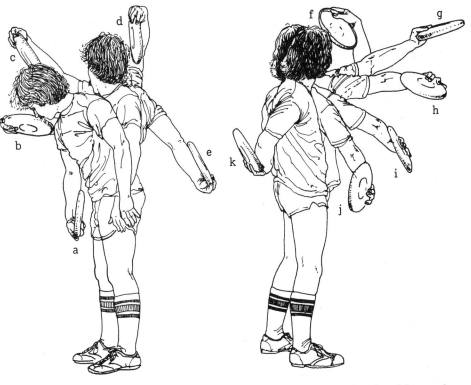

The angles of delivery for the overhand family. Closed stance: (a) cross-body gym-floor curve, (b) water skip, (c) cross-body upside-down, (d) roller, (e) a cocked position for skips and skip curves. Open stance: (f) overhead upside-down, (g) roll curve, (h) level flight, (i) skip, (j) multiple skips, (k) btb upside-down (a short-range toss which must be thrown from a stooped position).

There is an experimental variation—the extended grip. The thumb tugs against the cheek, while the forefinger and little finger push against the lip. The two middle fingers go on top.

If you're new to the owf delivery and are having a hard time visualizing it, try it this way: hold the belly of the disc to your backside (using a wrist-flip grip, of course). Raise your arm up, keeping it behind the plane of the body, then curve it forward into a level stroke. Normally, the wrist is level with the shoulder during the stroke, and the elbow is held just a smidgen higher than the shoulder and wrist. However, you can deliver a level wrist-flip flight with the arm in any position from just below horizontal to almost perfectly vertical, a feature which makes it very valuable in ultimate for getting a pass off over a defending player's reach.

As you turn toward a blind stance, the forearm gains more freedom to move independently of the whole arm, so more power can be achieved with less motion. For instance, in a regular open stance, an owf roll curve must be delivered with the disc

The wrist flip is prized in freestyle not only for its gliding flight and its graceful delivery but also for the many body motions it blends with. The wrist flip can be launched while leaping, crouching, pivoting, running . . .

entirely unlocked from the forearm. Consequently, the throw is all arm, little wrist, and pretty weak. If you turn halfway toward a blind stance, you can get a lot more spin on the throw.

Still, owf roll curves are incapable of producing long rolls. Most often, owf rollers are delivered this way: twist the forearm all the way around and coil the arm up over the shoulder. Reliably accurate curve rollers can be achieved from that position for the same reason that position produces accurate upside-down backhands: the stroke is made with the arm moving along the limit of its ability to flex further outward, which automatically grooves the stroke. As you might gather, if full twisting of the arm is needed to get a curve roller, getting a veer roller or even a straight roller can be a terrifically strenuous chore. Make the simple adjustment to a thumber grip to get the full range of roller release angles but with the loss of the automatically grooved stroke.

The owf blind throw utilizes that same free movement of the forearm. There is a version of the owf blind throw (in fact, the most common version) that begins with a normal forward stroke, which then turns and becomes a blind stroke over the shoulder. I call the throw a two-arm, after the three-arm backhand throw. However, a few very supple players can add a third dimension—throwing the disc forward again all the way around the neck. The name "three-arm" is already taken, so what would you call a three-arm wrist flip?

Wrist flips may lack a little when it comes to rolls, but they are outstanding performers on the skip side. The wrist flip gets even better skip banks than the sidearm is capable of. The throw is indis-

The first half of the upside-down stroke should be made with the forearm flipping over the elbow at a right angle to the upper arm. When the forearm reaches vertical, the entire arm extends out toward release.

pensable in golf for getting around big trees. Skip curves come quite naturally, as do skips and multiple skips. With multiple skips and gym-floor curves, you can get a giant "C" curve (right-handed), and, with a cross-body delivery of a gym-floor curve, you can get a tightly winding "S" curve (again,

A level wrist flip can be thrown with the arm in elevated positions simply by adjusting the wrist down.

The delivery position for multiple skips and gym-floor curves. If you use little arm and put enough spin on the disc, you can get it to come to a stop, then roll back to you.

An overhand delivery is ideal for bicycle Frisbee. Many throws have to be modified for use on a bicycle because their usual motion of delivery disrupts the ride. The motion of a wrist-flip, however, blends well with the motion of the bike.

right-handed). Angle the cross-body delivery upward just a bit to get what is probably the most wildly looping barrel-roll.

Wrist flips are also sturdy performers upside down. The delivery of an upside-down wrist flip can be made overhead or cross-body. The cross-body version is popular in freestyle because it can be thrown so that it settles down gently, almost like a hover.

A push throw is possible with a wrist-flip grip, just as with a backhand, but is delivered cross-body instead. The wrist-flip push has not, however,

A two-arm wrist flip. The throw starts forward, then turns back over the shoulder. As with the cross-body blind sidearm, this throw is often begun in an open stance with a pivot to the blind stance.

proven as handy as the backhand push. Another rare wrist-flip toss you might enjoy testing is a sort of underarmed version of the overhead upside-down throw. Simply double your arm up and hold the disc cocked under the upper arm. Fling the disc out from there using the same angle of release as the other upside-down wrist-flip throws.

Overhand wrist flips are very important in freestyle, golf, and ultimate. They are not often seen in guts or the field events. (Irv Kalb, a ceaseless inventor of Frisbee techniques, devised a way to disguise a thumber as an overhand wrist flip. The throw, which he called the in-flip, began as a wrist flip, but flipped over in mid-stroke to finish as a thumber. The idea was to lull the opposing guts team into expecting a cream-puff throw, then sock them with the thumber. However, getting power into the thumber after the flip was more of a problem than had been anticipated, and the throw was abandoned for guts. It's still a clever throw, one well worth trying.)

The upside-down wrist flip is the most prevalent upside-down throw in freestyle.

5. Hook-Thumb Family

The hook-thumb family is relatively new; nevertheless, they make up a complete family of throws. It is, however, a mysterious and unruly family that is just beginning to gain devotees.

The difficulty is the hook thumbers' incomparably high tendency to turn over. The stubbiest lever of all, the thumb, goes against the cheek and delivers the throw. In a thumber, the thumb provides leverage from its tip to the middle of the wrist. In a hook thumber, on the other hand, the thumb provides only about half that leverage— from the tip of the thumb to the knuckle. Furthermore, the more fingers you move up onto the flight plate to steady the grip, the more you limit the movement of the thumb and wrist.

So, hook thumbers are usually gripped by the rim alone. The extreme is the pinch grip, in which the rim is merely clamped between the thumb (laid along the cheek) and the forefinger (laid along the lip, but bent at the joint knuckle). It is a flimsy grip that requires excessive pressure and a very precise stroke if wobble is to be avoided. The two-finger hook-thumb grip, the one analogous to the two-finger sidearm grip, has the thumb opposing the middle finger, which is laid full-length along the lip, with the forefinger pressing on the flight plate just above the rim.

Turnover flights are the one area where hook thumbers are fairly well established. The barrel-roll hook thumber is delivered with a sidearm stroke that starts wide, scoops down, and is released with

A hook-thumb grip.

The pinch grip.

The cocked position for a question-mark curve.

64

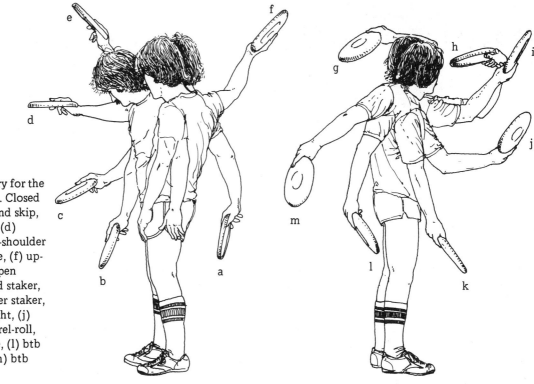

The angles of delivery for the hook-thumb family. Closed stance: (a) underhand skip, (b) skip, (c) staker, (d) cross-body over-the-shoulder staker, (e) roll curve, (f) upside-down flight. Open stance: (g) overhead staker, (h) over-the-shoulder staker, (i) upside-down flight, (j) mid-stroke of a barrel-roll, (k) gym-floor curve, (l) btb gym-floor curve, (m) btb staker.

the hand hypersupinated (bent all the way back). That throw has found a home in guts (see chapter 9). The hook-thumb gym-floor curve is the most spectacular of all gym-floor curves and is unfailingly accurate at a certain range. It is called the question-mark curve, because it follows a "?" configuration viewed from a right-handed thrower's perspective.

The barrel-roll and the question-mark curve can be thrown behind the back, forward and back-ward between the legs, blind, as well as with the sidearm delivery. The barrel-roll, I should add, can be thrown as a very extraordinary skip shot.

For some reason, level hook-thumb deliveries have come to be known as stakers, a rather nice name. Though stakers have been common knowledge for about four years, only a handful of players use them with any regularity. Senior World Champion Ed Headrick frequently employs stakers in his freestyle play with totally reliable accuracy

The release position for a
cross-body staker.

Also, with that grip, the staker can be thrown from virtually any position of the arm: underhand, over the onside shoulder, overhead, cross-body over the shoulder, and cross-body. And those throws can be made from closed, facing, and open stances. That gives the staker some unique possibilities for quick returns in freestyle.

And, of course, the hook thumber offers the full complement of curves, skips, rollers, hovers, blind throws, and upside-down throws. The upside-down hook thumber is exceedingly prone to wobble. Careful attention to a firm grip and a direct stroke, however, can do away with the wobble and give you a very handy throw.

The staker holds some possibility as a distance throw, probably not for distance competition, but as a useful throw in golf, for instance. While the staker may be in the course of being broken in for use at moderate range, it's still a wild and untamed thing for distance. Thirty-nine distance attempts will flop over like a flapjack, but the fortieth will fly like a bird, demonstrating that the potential is there somewhere.

The mark of advanced players is the way they move with ease from catch to throw without fumbling around adjusting grips or making up their minds what grip to use. Almost always, such dexterity with grips is learned secondarily during the course of thousands of throws. However, it is a skill that can be learned quite readily with practice.

Now that you are through this chapter, you

and control. His example, along with that of a few others, has helped renew interest in the staker among players who had dismissed it as too unreliable.

A recent innovation in the hook-thumb grip has tamed the staker quite a bit and also should insure that stakers will be much more popular in the future. By opposing the thumb with both the index and middle fingers laid full-length along the lip, the leverage of the thumb is extended all the way to the wrist, and the wrist, in turn, can produce the whippier bye-bye motion. Turnover tendency is significantly reduced.

should have a working familiarity with the major grips. Drill on changing smoothly and quickly from any one grip to any other. Figure out how to go through the following sequence of grips, working with only one hand at a time: thumber to sidearm to hook thumber to thumber to backhand to wrist flip to sidearm to hook thumber to backhand. Go back through in reverse sequence. Once you've got it pat one way, go through and figure out a variation for each adjustment. Go through it letting the disc leave the hand and without letting go of the disc.

Obviously, the adjustments that require only a shift of the disc (backhand—sidearm, hook thumber—wrist flip) are easiest. Several deceptive throws are based on those shifts. Fake a two-arm throw and, when the disc shifts, come forward with a cross-body staker. Or, fake a blind staker and bring the arm back around for a two-arm throw. On a cross-body trailing-edge catch (see chapter 11), bring the return backhand all the way around until the disc shifts, then throw a sidearm. There are all sorts of these disguised throws you can figure out.

There is one staker throw that creates a spectacular illusion. It begins in a meditational position, then bursts into a flurry of seemingly impossible activity. Cock your staker around so that your fingernails touch the center of your chest. Bring your other arm up and duplicate the grip from the opposite direction. Meditate awhile; then, to throw, fling both arms straight out. The secret is to let loose of the grip with the nonthrowing hand right away, but to keep the hand close to the action.

The release position for an upside-down hook thumber.

A btb staker with a pinch grip. With almost any other delivery, the angle of release shown here would produce a skip. For a hook thumber, however, particularly with a pinch grip, that is the hyzer necessary for a level flight.

6. Catapults

The distinguishing feature of catapults is that they are launched by one finger laid along the cheek of the disc. The forefinger is most widely preferred, but the middle finger also gives good results. And each of the other two fingers or even the thumb may be used, though with a falling off in form and power. One finger alone, however, is not sufficient to catapult the disc two meters. A mechanism for holding the disc steady for aiming and for the even application of power during the launch is necessary. If, for instance, you wanted to catapult the disc straight up, gravity would serve to steady the disc against your finger. Or, if you begin a throwing stroke with a one-finger sidearm grip and drop the thumb away, you still have the force of acceleration to keep the disc steady. What is actually used as the steadying mechanism in almost all cases is a cuff, and catapults do feature the most elaborate cuffs in Frisbee.

A cuff serves also to pull the disc back against the finger, flexing the finger for extra power. However, in the backhand catapult, the granddaddy of all catapults, beginners often run into trouble when drawing back on the disc. The lip of the disc must ride between the knuckles of the forefinger and middle finger. (See top photo, this column.) The middle knuckle plays an indispensable role in locking the disc into the grip, and that's where beginners have trouble. The trick, very simply, is to turn your hand back into the disc so that the disc catches on the middle knuckle and does not slide across the back of the hand. Beginners also tend to get the various catapult grips confused, which is understandable given the diversity and novelty of these throws. If catapults are new to you, pick up a disc

The standard grip for a backhand catapult. Bending the launching finger slightly, as shown here, helps to exert more pressure against the cheek.

No standard sidearm catapult grip has emerged yet, but this one seems to be the most common. Hook the disc on your forefinger, roll it back against the base of the thumb, and cuff it with your other thumb.

and try out the different grips as you read this chapter.

Catapults are no mere wind egg; you can produce any flight with a catapult that is possible with any other family of throws—curves, skips, rollers, upside-down, hovers. Only gym-floor curves and barrel rolls come off weak. Except for that minor shortcoming, catapults offer more than sufficient accuracy, range, and versatility for freestyle. Their one drawback for freestyle lies in the time it takes to set up the rather intricate grips.

All catapults fall into two divisions: backhand and sidearm. In both cases the palm is turned out from the thrower. Power comes from the forward flip of the wrist and finger, with some assistance from the forearm. In the backhand grip, the disc rests on the inner side of the forefinger and locks against the back of the hand; in the sidearm grip it rests on the outer side of the forefinger and locks against the base of the thumb on the back side of the hand. Beyond that, differences in catapults are rather cosmetic, the result of numerous ways to

A finger flip with a bth cuff, one of several intricate positions this catapult can be delivered from. The sidearm version is pictured here. A backhand is achieved simply by laying the launching finger in the other direction along the cheek.

The cocked position for a level backhand catapult (left) and for an upside-down backhand catapult (right). Catapults can fly twenty meters or more with just the power of the wrist and finger. With the added power of an arm swing, flights of more than forty meters are possible. The thrower in these two pictures is getting ready to put a good deal of arm into the launch.

cuff catapults, using everything from teeth to toes, and I'll leave it to you to come up with as many as you like.

To get level flight you have to put hyzer on the disc during delivery. In the backhand catapult that means getting your elbow up higher than your hand. From that position you turn the forearm down just about as far as it will comfortably go to get the correct hyzer for a skip shot. Lay your forearm back over your elbow as far as it will go the other way to get your arms in the proper position to deliver an upside-down throw. (To get the rest of your body in position, change from a closed to an open stance.) The position for rollers and roll curves is about halfway between skip and upside down. Just as delivery angles for the backhand catapult match those of backhand throws, the delivery angles for the sidearm catapult match those of forehand throws.

There are two catapults that don't quite fit the mold: the finger flip and the spinner. Dr. Johnson

Creative players can come up with endless ways to cuff their catapults. When using this head cuff, remember that hair offers much less friction than skin does. You can cuff the disc with your nose, teeth, forearm, palm, toes, as well as with the side of a building, a tree trunk, another Frisbee, your co-oping partner. . .

describes the finger flip on page 52 of his book. It differs from other catapults in that the disc is not locked back against the hand. In fact, one finger of each hand is all that touches the disc—the launching finger at the nose and the cuffing finger at the tail. It can be thrown as a backhand or as a sidearm; it can also be thrown behind the head, blind, between the legs, plus a few other ways. Finally, it has value in freestyle because it follows naturally from an inside freeze (see chapter 12) and from a two-finger pick up (see chapter 16), not to mention all the many graceful arm movements it lends itself to.

The steadying mechanism of the spinner is the spinning of the disc about the finger—it is the cuffless catapult. (Similarly, you can catapult a disc off a delay. See chapter 14.) The disc is propelled by a well-timed whip of the finger. (You can make this throw with your Frisbee stick as well. See chapter 14.) The throw can be made sidearm or backhand with either spin, but it only works well as a sidearm and with spin that carries the disc forward in the lower portion of its revolution (right spin for the right hand, left for the left). Most players regard the throw as a curiosity for use at short ranges, but spinners have been thrown in the sixty-meter range and accurate throws at thirty meters should, with practice, be within the ability of most players. All it takes is timing. To develop timing, count off the revolutions and throw on the same revolution each time—three, five, ten, whatever. Begin mod-

A bth backhand catapult. At close range this throw can be executed in such a way that the catcher can see no arm movement and cannot even see the Frisbee until it comes shooting around the neck.

estly, though. Throw on the first spin and at a range of only five meters or so. Build up from there.

The spinner is as unruly a throw as any in Frisbee, but even it will respond to dedicated practice. You can even learn to throw skips and blind shots with it. The angle of delivery for a level flight is shown here.

One of the most mystical evenings of my life centered around spinners. On a walk one autumn night in 1969, I saw a player make a finger spinning catch and return a spinner to his partner. The technique was not new to me, but I had never seen it executed with such authority (and haven't since). As I watched, he made a succession of about fifteen spinning catches, each followed by a spinner. The glow of the Moonlighter he played with had its usual eerie effect as it spun on his finger, but what held me spellbound was the uncanny accuracy of the throws he winged back to his partner, who was almost invisible to me in the darkness. Through all those exchanges, this player held perfect control of the disc with only one finger. I never saw the player again, never met him, but I remember him clearly. The memory of that moment is otherworldly. It is certainly the same rare crystal-clear glimpse of athletic perfection described by Michael Murphy in *Golf in the Kingdom* and by George Leonard in *The Ultimate Athlete*. In the years since that evening I've often experienced that sensation of perfection, during my own play and while watching other players. It's the sensation of flying I spoke of in chapter 1, and those spinners that evening were my introduction to that sensation.

7. Odds & Ends

This is the chapter for all those throws that don't fit into the other categories. Almost without exception, their only use is for short-range passes. Still, there are all sorts of occasions when short, fancy flips are called for—indoors, or when playing with very young children. Say your Frisbee falls halfway between you and your partner, you retrieve it, and you are then standing only about ten meters from your partner. What throw do you use? You can use your backhand or sidearm, but at that range they require only a flip of the wrist. Nothing showy in that. Better to use a throw you can really put some effort into. And some of the throws in this chapter will take all the effort you can give them and still not fly ten meters.

The oddest of the odd are the throws that are gripped not by the rim but by the flight plate—the spider and its variations. Lay the disc on the upturned fingers of your throwing hand so that the belly of the disc rests on the fingertips (you can also lay the back of the disc on your fingertips for an upside-down flight). Flip the wrist around and the forearm forward to launch the throw. Also, lift your hand slightly upward as you move it forward in order to increase friction between your fingers and the disc. The spider, when thrown as just described, has an effective range of only four or five meters. However, with a 97G, a Regular, a Pro, or a 119 G, if your hand is large enough, you can cheat a little by spreading your fingertips out to the rim. The improved grip will quadruple your range, and it can be used for a few trick throws, such as a three-arm spider or an upside-down throw from an inverted grip.

The pizza is a spider with the disc laid flat on the hand. Like the spider, it won't go far unless you cheat. Sling the disc off your little finger

A sidearm sandwich throw. To get maximum power, place the little finger of your lower hand up against the cheek. The sandwich throw can also be made as a backhand, using roughly the same motion you would use to heave water out of a bucket.

73

(sidearm version) or thumb (backhand version) to get more distance. The spider and the pizza perform best when both hands are used. The second hand is placed on top of the disc, usually in a mirror image of the lower hand. A two-handed spider is called a double spider, and a two-handed pizza is called a sandwich throw or a hamburger throw.

I have yet to learn of a common name for the next throw. I call it a spin-off, but there is probably a more common name lurking around somewhere. Place your hands on either side of the disc, fingers pointed upward, and press the disc between both sets of fingers (this is the freeze position discussed in chapter 12). Rotate the disc around the spin axis clockwise or counterclockwise until one hand is at the nose and the other is at the tail. The throw is best launched from overhead, but may also be launched from chest level or from over one shoulder or the other. Press tightly enough to bend the disc slightly. To send the disc on its way, spin it out of your hands as you would a set up but with a forward motion of the hands, particularly the rear

The spin of a spin-off throw is determined by which way the arms are crossed. With the left hand on the tail of the disc, as shown here, the disc flies with left spin. It can also be thrown with hands inverted, but with a falling off in distance and accuracy.

hand. With the right hand on the tail, you get right spin; with the left hand on the tail, you get left spin. I've seen this throw travel about twenty meters, but ten meters is a more reasonable expectation.

A spider that borrows something from the spin-off is the outside spider, which is simply a spider with fingers clutching the outside of the disc. To my knowledge it has only been performed with the Mini-Frisbee and discs of comparable size, but, who knows, maybe there's a player somewhere whose fingers will fit around a Regular or even a Pro. Unlike other spiders, the outside spider can be thrown rightside-up in an inverted position. The double outside spider has one hand in the normal position and one in the inverted position, with fingers interlocked.

Another grip pretty much limited to the Mini is the scissor grip. Clamp the Mini by the rim between

The rare outside spider is one of the more reliable grips for a Mini-Frisbee.

forefinger and middle finger (or any other two fingers) with the arm and hand in a backhand position. Throw as you would a backhand. The scissor grip can be delivered sidearm as well, but not as satisfactorily.

As most players usually discover for themselves, a Frisbee can be hurled like a discus. However, a saucer lacks the steadying mass of a discus and, so,

The butterfly. The disc is perched up on the thumb upside down (left). The throw is made by pushing forward and downward with the fingers against the edge of the disc.

The paper-plane grip is a cousin of the snap thumber grip. Throw the disc as you would a paper plane, or flick the ring and little fingers to fling the disc to your offside, or flick the index and middle fingers to sail the disc behind your head, or push away from you with the thumb for a butterfly.

tends to squirm around in your hand as you pivot around for the throw. The grip can be improved by wedging the disc in place with the forearm. The backhand version of this throw is discussed in the next chapter and is, in fact, called the wedge. The hammer also gets its name from its similarity to a track and field event—the hammer throw, obviously. Usually, it is a sidearm with the free hand clamped down to cover the thumb of the throwing hand one way or another, to give the comic impression of hurling a great weight. As such it belongs in the forehand chapter rather than here, but there is a variation that belongs here. Hold the disc in a pinch grip with your nonpreferred hand, replace the thumb with the index and middle fingers of the throwing hand, then wrap the thumb around those two fingers. Throw as you would a staker.

The butterfly, as well as being an eye-catching short-range pass, finds use in golf and freestyle. To throw, push your arm forward and downward, making the disc flip end over end. Because the arm

pushes pretty much straight ahead, the throw is very accurate. Obviously, however, the disc is not going to go very far—seven or eight meters at most, half that into a wind—but that's just what you often want in a golf putt.

Hold a disc out in front of you with a sidearm grip. Swing the outside edge of the disc up a little, then thrust sharply downward with your thumb, leaving the disc flipping end over end in mid-air. Catch whichever of the two flipping edges you can, using the same two-finger grip. If you catch the edge that's turning over edge-first, you'll have a sidearm grip again. If you catch the edge coming over back-first, you'll have a hook-thumb grip. Either way, flip the disc up again several more times until you are used to this little toss, which is known as a flip-up butterfly. Use it for a little razzle-dazzle in your freestyle. Flip one up and throw a sidearm or question-mark curve right after you catch it. You can also use it in trick positions—behind the back, between the legs, under a leg, and so forth.

If you have a disc hovering in front of you after a tip or a set up, you can send it flying to your partner by giving it a slap on its tail in the direction of its spin. The technique is called brushing and is discussed in chapter 15. Hold the disc out in front of you on the fingertips of your nonpreferred hand and give it a slap. Try it that way a few times before attempting it with the disc spinning. One variation that children love is the head slap. Set a disc on your head and send it sailing with a brush.

By now most people who are at all interested in Frisbee play have heard that you can throw a disc with your foot. Actually, you can throw one with your foot two different ways. Anybody who can pinch their big toe together with the one next to it can throw it this way: lay the disc over the top of your foot and pinch the rim between your toes so that your big toe presses against the lip and your other toes are under the disc. Stand in an open stance, lift your foot a few inches off the ground and cock it back some, then give a swift forward kick to send it flying. The other method is a bit more powerful and also more difficult to master. Lay the Frisbee across your foot again, pinching the rim between your toes, but this time with the big toe under the disc, against the cheek. Kick your leg sharply around behind you to launch the disc. I say this method is more powerful than the other, but that is only true when it is in the hands (feet?) of two or three players who have perfected this delivery.

After you have practiced all these throws individually, try your hand at close-up freestyle. Stand only eight or ten meters apart from your partner and get a freestyle routine going at a brisk pace using the throws in this chapter and a few others, such as pushes, the spinner, the three-arm, and, of course, the various air bounces. Close-up freestyle is a superb way to sharpen your reflexes—it's much more challenging than you might think.

The foot throw is capable of distances in the thirty meter range with a fair degree of accuracy. The trick is to start the foot forward smoothly and slowly. Accelerate rapidly to get off a good swift kick.

8. Air Bounces

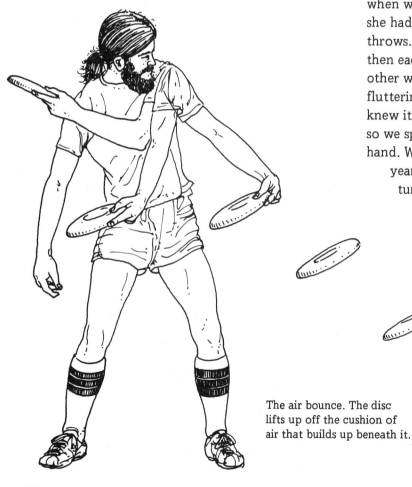

One fall day back in 1968 a young player joined a few of us old veterans out on the mall. Every time she backhanded the disc to us it would swoop down slightly just after release, then rise up to a perfectly accurate flight. She was a little puzzled when we asked how she was getting the disc to dip: she hadn't noticed anything different about her throws. We watched her from close up for a while, then each of us vets took a try at it. One after another we plowed the disc into the ground or sent it fluttering stupidly over our heads. After that, we knew it must be something she was doing wrong, so we spent twenty minutes correcting her backhand. What a chance we were missing! In all the years since then I've seen only four other natural air bouncers—players who put an air bounce into their backhand the first time they throw it. How incredible that we failed to pick up on what she was doing and especially that we would teach her not to!

The air bounce. The disc lifts up off the cushion of air that builds up beneath it.

78

The silhouette of the thumb indicates how far back the thumb should go for a proper backhand air-bounce grip.

The importance of the backhand air bounce cannot be overstated. Most of the better freestylers use it. Many use it for eighty percent or more of their throws at a stretch. The backhand air bounce is fairly simple to learn if you keep one important point in mind, and that is this: you begin a normal backhand with the thumb pointed away from the target. The thumb swings around through 180° and ends up pointing toward the target at release.

You begin a backhand air bounce with the thumb pointed away from the target also (and slightly upward), but then you roll it down and through the throw. The thumb doesn't kick around to give the

disc spin until just the instant before release, and even then it happens so automatically that you don't really need to worry about it. Concentrate instead on rolling that thumb straight through toward the target.

If you are just starting to learn air bounces, you may find the shoulder air bounce the best place to begin. Simply lay the tail of the disc on your throwing shoulder. Apply pressure with your thumb so that the disc will pop down as soon as you slide it off your shoulder. Once you get the hang of that, start lifting up on your back leg and then dropping all your weight down as you deliver the disc. You can get tremendous bounces off your shoulder because the motion of the arm is almost totally in a downward direction and because the

downward thrust of the body helps build a great deal of upward pressure under the disc. You can throw shoulder bounces with full might but in such a way that they barely make it to your partner standing only five or six meters away. But what a flight in between!

Once you master the shoulder bounce, you can usually go on to master the backhand air bounce in less than twenty or thirty attempts. Actually,

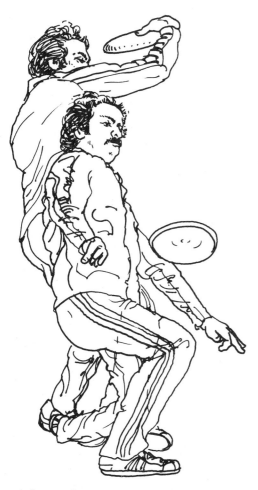

you'll just be getting the hang of it; complete mastery may take several weeks or months. If you find you aren't having much success learning air bounces, simply try tossing the disc down flat a meter or so in front of you. When you start scattering leaves with your throws, you're getting a bounce. After that, just lean back a little and your bounces will start flying off toward your partner. If that fails, try throwing the disc with a level

When an air bounce is thrown from over the on-side shoulder, the downward motion is so sharp that the bounce is exaggerated, doubly so when the body drops down as well.

A backhand air bounce. The fingers point downward at release. Compare the position of the hand in the drawing of a backhand delivery on page 42.

In a regular backhand (a) the arm comes straight around. In a backhand air bounce (b) the arm rolls the disc downward.

stroke but with thirty degrees or so of positive attitude on it. At least that way you should get the feel of an air bounce.

Air bounces hold forth limitless possibilities. With a slight downward slap of the disc during delivery (a beavertail), you can send it sailing along with a shallow dip to help take some of the edge off the forward momentum of the disc. Fling the disc down with some force; it will duck down, then zip right up into a hover. Jam it down with all your might, and it will slam to a shuddering standstill, then climb haltingly up. Lean into the bounce to send the disc scurrying shin high all the way to your partner.

It's worth pointing out that you don't have to throw the disc down at the ground to get an air bounce. You can throw bounces to either side or even upside down. I've found a roll-bank air bounce handy every now and then in golf for get-ting around fat obstacles. You can throw an air bounce upside down by throwing an upside-down backhand and rolling your thumb upward and through the delivery. If you throw an air bounce with a level stroke straight at your partner with a stiff wind at your back, the disc will "tail skate" all the way. To some extent you can get the disc to bounce when thrown down topside first, though of course a lot of pressure is lost without the rim down to hold it in.

A very pretty freestyle move is the blind air bounce. Hold the disc shoulder high in front of you, then swoop it straight back behind you. Usually, though, a blind air bounce is begun in the closed stance. The thrower pivots to the offside as the disc is started forward, then releases the disc in mid-pivot.

The only requirement for air bouncing is that you have a firm grip with enough surface area of the hand in position to push the disc into the bounce. Obviously, the other fan grip, the wrist-flip grip, is adequate, but a wrist-flip air bounce is a little more complicated than a backhand air bounce because a change in the direction of the arm's movement is necessary in mid-stroke.

Get a disc and hold it straight out from your shoulder as if you were in mid-stroke of an owf delivery. Raise your elbow just a fraction, then pop it down, keeping your wrist level with your shoulder the entire time. Notice how the disc also pops down. Push down on the disc some with your last

Co-ordinating the movements of an owf air bounce takes some practice. Pay particular attention to the position of the arm, hand, and fingers at release.

three fingers, lean forward and down from the waist, and lower your arm halfway down. You've just gone through the motions necessary for getting a good solid air bounce with an overhand wrist flip. If you just want a slight dip in the flight, you can get it by popping the elbow or scooping with the fingers or both.

Starting a wrist flip from the top of the throw is a little difficult. You'll still need to begin by raising your arm from behind your back as usual. Better timing is required, but it's worth it. The graceful, wavelike motion of the arm in an owf air bounce is one of the most beautiful moves in freestyle.

There are several oddball ways to get an air bounce. A hook-thumb grip with two or three fingers moved well back on top of the disc can give you an air bounce, but it will be wobbly because the hand is not in a very good position to impart spin. As far as I know, no one has ever been able to get anything resembling an air bounce with a side-arm grip, but I do know one player who every now and then can get a bounce with a three-arm throw, something of a feat! You can sometimes get a very short-range air bounce with a scoop (see chapter

15) by twisting the hand to give the disc spin.

Similar to the scoop is the wedge, which, as mentioned in the previous chapter, is the backhand cousin of the discus throw. To get a firm enough grip, the disc must be wedged (that's where it gets its name) between the fingers and the skin of the forearm. It's a throw worth practicing because it makes a very impressive short-range pass. (The wedge with a Mini-Frisbee becomes the inverted palm grip.)

Air bounces are the best throws to work with for learning discwork and advanced catches. They are better than throws that are merely thrown softly because they move with more uniform speed, carry more spin, and are less prone to slide off course. For learning discwork, have your partner set you up with "toys"—hovering bounces that spin like the dickens. In a brisk wind you can set up your own toys by sending an air bounce down at your toes. It will tower right in front of you, rising up perfect for tipping, brushing, delaying, whatever.

The wedge can produce a strong air bounce. Bind the disc in between the palps of the fingers and a fold of skin on the forearm to get a secure grip.

9. Distance & Power

Before you start throwing with all your might, there are some things you need to do. First, bend over and see if you can touch your palms to the floor with your legs straight. If you can't, start trying. Find some good stretching exercises for your arms, back, and legs. Do a few push-ups and sit-ups and some light weightlifting with your wrists and arms. Maintain a daily exercise program. If you can already touch your palms to the floor, you probably have been keeping in shape. Keep it up.

The second thing to do is to spend several days a week for several weeks freestyling at moderate range. Work to develop consistent accuracy with backhands, sidearms, and wrist flips at thirty to forty meters or more, using several different types of flight for each throw.

After working on these other areas, spend three straight days doing this: when you go out to play, run through some warm-up exercises for your back

Backhand power grips. (a) The Clarke-Shelton grip represents an early attempt to get more reach into the backhand delivery. The middle two fingers pull against the cheek. (b) The May grip also has longer reach as its purpose. The May grip was used in the first throw to travel ninety yards. However, both it and the Clarke-Shelton grips have disappeared from distance competition because problems in getting a strong, steady release more than offset the advantage of longer reach. (c) The fist grip or Berkeley power grip gets more use in guts than in distance. (d) A modified fist grip is now most commonly used for distance. The palps of the fingers, instead of gripping against the cheek, press on the flight plate where they can provide more control of flight attitude. The classic backhand grip is not well suited for distance because the forefinger gets in the way.

and shoulders. One of the best for your shoulders is to rotate your arms in small and then in large circles, one direction and then the other, palm up and palm down, straight out to your sides and then straight out in front of you. Spend thirty or forty minutes freestyling, then throw about a dozen throws for distance with backhand or sidearm. Push yourself just past about three-quarters power at first. Shoot for consistent distance somewhere between forty and sixty meters, whatever is most appropriate for you. I would strongly recommend that you take a dozen Frisbee discs of the same model (even the same mold number, if possible) with you. You need to make one throw after the next without being distracted by the different flight properties of the various models or by having to fetch discs or to wait for your partner to return them.

After each throw, concentrate on ways to improve the next throw. When you decide on a change in your delivery, walk through the throw a few times with the change inserted until you blend the new with the old. When it feels right, throw it. Decide which ways gave the best results, then throw your last three throws that same way, using all the power you can without upsetting the flight of the disc and without disturbing your timing. After you've thrown your dozen throws, make some mental notes on what you can do to improve.

There are three reasons for all this preparation besides the obvious one of wanting your arm and body in shape to throw. First, you should start actual distance practice by setting a standard for judging your future improvement. You might even try recording the distances of your throws. If you set your standard with your arm in shape, you can be more certain that improvements in your throwing distance are a result of improved technique, not simply of better muscle response.

Second, because distance throwing requires lots and lots of drill on small portions of the overall motion, you need to have a good feel for that motion. If you want to work just on getting the right tug in your shoulder at the top of the backswing, for instance, you need to be able to feel where your arm should be naturally, without having to go through the entire windup each time. Also, this chapter will make much more sense if you can relate it to your own manner of throwing.

Third, you need to have respect for distance and power. Done properly, they can be excellent exercise and can directly benefit many other playing skills. They can also, if not treated with respect, give you a lot of pain and can ruin other areas of your game. Throw in moderation. Soreness will be your best instructor, but, particularly in the learning stages, don't wait for the soreness to show before you stop throwing. Throw no more than a dozen power throws a day at first, then wait to see if appreciable soreness develops. If it does, you know you're doing something wrong or else you've got a few muscles that need more exercise. If you don't feel much soreness, you can push your power a little the next day and maybe throw a few more throws too. It's like getting a suntan in the spring:

you don't have to wait for it to start hurting to know you're tanning, but you soon learn how much sun you can take without doing yourself harm.

And there is another very good reason for not attempting more than a dozen high-powered throws a day, or even that many if you don't think about what you are doing. When you do something the same way several times, you are learning it, correct or not. When you work on your distance, you should be looking to find the ingredients of a successful throw, not practicing to ingrain your early mistakes. For now, work to figure out ways to change and improve each throw. You are months away from constant practice of one single manner of delivery.

Four different delivery styles are most often used in guts: backhands, usually thrown with a roll hyzer, are used for their controlled accuracy; side-

A guts thumber (above) and a guts sidearm (right). Notice in both how the back leg is used to push the body forward, how the forward arm leads the rotation of the body, and how far around the shoulders get at release.

arms are thrown for their lethal speed; thumbers get a high burst of speed and carry a lot of spin; and barrel-roll hook thumbers are increasing in popularity because their unstable, screwball flights are difficult for catchers to zero in on.

With power throws you have to build consistent accuracy and then use that control as a channel for increasing your power. One tip that will help: begin your throwing stroke at half speed and accelerate to greater speed. Increase the throwing speed only if you can maintain accuracy, but always use

steady acceleration in your delivery. You might want to set up a target for practice. Guts throws generally fly in the 90-mile-an-hour range, but an occasional one will hit the speed traps at 110. Most of the following principles for increasing distance will also be of use in improving guts power.

Distance throwing in general requires the production of maximum linear velocity in the object you are throwing. Velocity is a product of force and time, which means the greater the force or the longer you can apply the force, the greater the velocity of the disc at release. Slowing down your arm will gain time, but it will also decrease the amount of force. Time is increased by getting maximum length of the stroke for a given radius (the radius in Frisbee throwing is the distance from the center of the disc to your body's axis of rotation). Applied to distance throwing, that means approaching the throwing line turned slightly toward a blind stance so that you can maximize your backswing and the coil of your body. In the delivery it means uncoiling your shoulders and hips all the way around just before the moment of release. Every millimeter of stretch you can get out of your muscles will help.

As you hold your arm straight and sweep it around you, the fingers obviously move faster than the wrist, which moves faster than the elbow, and so on. The further out along the radius, the greater the velocity. The more body weight you can distribute out away from the axis of rotation while maintaining the velocity, the greater the momentum you will impart to the disc when you release it. To achieve maximum momentum, get as many parts of your body as possible rotating in the direction of the throw—your nonthrowing arm, your free leg, even your head. However, getting any object to start rotating is made more difficult the more its mass is distributed away from the rotational axis. The compromise is to start your throwing motion with your weight in close but to lengthen the radius rapidly as you turn until you reach full radius at release.

Maximum force production depends on efficient use of the body's muscles and its levers. Swing your arm straight back. That tug you feel is the stretch reflex. If you start your arm forward with that tug, you'll get a boost in speed. If you don't, your arm becomes dead weight. Exercise can stretch the muscles so that you can get your arm further back before you experience the tug. However, that's not all there is to using your muscles efficiently. To gain maximum speed of rotation as you uncoil your body, start with the large muscles —buttocks, thigh, and lower back—then work to the chest and shoulders and on out to the arms, legs, wrist, and fingers. That means you have to put numerous stretch reflexes in timed sequence. Just how intricate a sequence will become clear in the next paragraph. Another thing to remember about muscles is that not all of them help in any given task. Muscles that work against the desired motion

must be relaxed. The more inappropriate movements you make, the more muscles you will have working that you don't want working. This will be much more of a problem for people who attempt distance throwing without working to build up from moderate range. But even an experienced distance thrower, when overly tense, will have tension build up in the antagonistic muscles. Relaxation exercises can be a big help. Close your eyes, draw a deep breath, and let your arms and body go limp for a few moments before throwing.

Get a disc and try this experiment: standing with both feet on the ground, swing through a level sidearm distance throw without releasing the disc. When you feel the stretch reflex in your backswing, start forward with your arm straight and with full power. Listen for the "whoosh." Do the same

Keith Moher prepares to unleash a barrel-roll hook-thumber guts throw.

thing again, only this time, when you bring your arm forward, throw the elbow ahead first. As the elbow comes down, your forearm is being cocked.

The pendulum swing is one of the favored backhand distance techniques. The hips turn away from the throwing line during the approach, then the leading leg thrusts forward to help begin the body's forward rotation. Notice that even the head moves around to add momentum to the throwing motion.

Whip the forearm through and then the wrist and fingers, moving each section of your arm in sequence. If you did this second delivery correctly, you heard a slightly higher pitched "whiish" that indicates the disc is moving at higher speed than in the swing before.

Your arm moves faster in the second instance for two reasons. First, instead of using your muscular force to move your whole arm, you are using it to move the upper arm and a fraction of the lower arm's weight. The upper arm moves faster and the lower arm begins moving enough that it is no longer dead weight. (A force works more efficiently on an object moving in the same direction as the force than on an object at rest.) Second, when the parts of the arm move in sequence, the muscles can exert more force because of more efficient use of the stretch reflex as well as better mechanical advantage. In effect, your arm acts as several levers, each deriving power from the ones before, rather than as a single lever. In this way, momentum is multiplied.

Now you can explore adding a walk-up or run-up to your delivery. The obvious purpose of a run-up is to add linear momentum to your movement and thus to the flight of the disc, but a run-up that does not blend smoothly into the rotational motion of your particular delivery style is of no value. Work back and forth from walk-up and run-up into delivery and delivery to walk-up. Also, a faulty backswing can negate much or even all of the momentum the run-up produces. The walk-up and delivery have to be worked into a well co-ordinated, fluid, reproducible whole. Another purpose of the walk-up is to stretch the muscles more prior to throwing, a sort of last second warm-up.

Something to keep in mind about a run-up: once your feet leave the ground, you cannot increase the momentum of your body and you cannot change the path of your center of gravity. Keep one leg on the ground as a drive leg to get forward thrust.

Don't be afraid to search for novel style in your distance throw. Think how many years high jumping had been around before Dick Fosbury came up with the flop. However, no new technique will succeed if it violates basic mechanical principles. And, on the other hand, you should always be on the lookout for elements of other players' styles you think might successfully adapt to and improve your own. If you do make a change in your delivery, you need to work it in until it becomes automatic. Even a minor change may need many hours of patient drill, and a major change may take days. Just keeping your delivery honed to high skill level will require an hour or more of practice at least every couple of days.

Only two throws are capable of producing the distances necessary for distance competition, and one of these is somewhat superior to the other. Most distance throwers use a backhand delivery. Only six or seven serious distance competitors use a sidearm delivery. At the time of this writing, both the indoor world record (277 feet) and the outdoor world record (412 feet) are owned by Dave Johnson and his cannonlike backhand. But

A slightly modified pendulum swing delivery. Notice the large step forward between figures 4 and 5 and the very full follow-through of both arms in figures 6 and 7.

1   2

the sidearm is the better throw—it just hasn't been quite perfected (though Victor Malafronte holds an unofficial world record of 420 feet with a sidearm). The sidearm is better for the following reasons:

- More positive grip. The fingers in a sidearm grip propel by pushing against the disc in the direction of flight, whereas in the backhand the main pressure of the fingers is perpendicular to the line of flight.
- Freer elbow movement. The elbow locks up past a certain point in backhand throws. In sidearm throws the forearm is free to follow through independently of the upper arm.
- Longer reach. A sidearm is thrown off the tip of the middle finger, while the backhand is gripped only at thumb length.
- The serape effect. The way the muscles of the chest are aligned (like the angular cut of a serape) can produce more force in forehand motion than in backhand.
- More force of rotation. In the backhand the throwing shoulder leads the rotation, but in a sidearm the forward leg and shoulder can be swung around to increase the force of body rotation before the throwing shoulder even starts forward. Also, once your forward leg swings behind you in a sidearm it acts as a counterbalance, allowing you to lean further into the throw. (A helpful drill for teaching proper rotation for sidearms is to throw two discs at once—a backhand with the leading arm just preceding the sidearm. Strive for force, not beauty, in the backhand, and throw it slightly behind you.)

Some things can be said for the backhand too. A

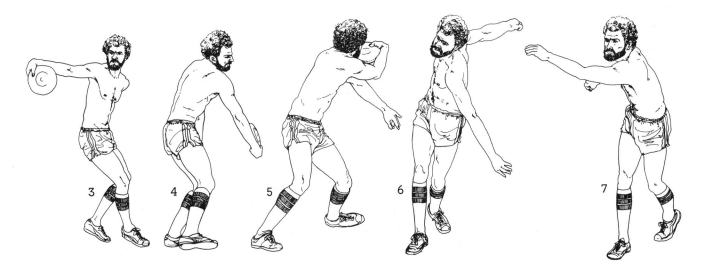

3   4   5   6   7

backhand puts greater spin on the disc at release—thus the disc is more stable in flight, less prone to fade off to one side or the other near the end of the flight. However, if all other factors of flight are equal (though no one can say they are), less spin would produce the greatest possible, if less consistent, distance because less energy of flight would be used up in the rotation of the disc.

Another advantage backhands offer is that the arm is close to the chest when rotation is begun. That allows body rotation to gain momentum more readily, but it is such an insignificant advantage that it is offset by other factors. Finally and most importantly, the backhand plays the wind better. With a backhand you can get the tail end of the disc jacked up a little higher (negative attitude) to catch more of the breeze. John Connelly's winning backhand distance throw in the 1976 World Frisbee Championship preliminaries got an amazing

The sidearm distance grip.

four or five inflection points because of the extreme negative attitude he was able to put on it. However, more of your hand is under the disc with a sidearm, which would seem to indicate that there is a way to get good negative attitude with a sidearm—it hasn't been discovered yet, but many people are working on it. The question is, can you

get that negative attitude without sacrificing power and without further decreasing stability?

Indoor distance throwing is simple. You aim for 278 feet, make your best throw, and whatever distance you get is a measure of how well you threw. Outdoor distance throwing has another dimension. You may have noticed that the outdoor world record was almost half again as long as the indoor record—135 feet longer. Those extra feet don't just come from having a following breeze; they come from experience in playing the wind.

Two breezes aren't the same just because they have the same speed. Even one breeze can vary from moment to moment and from one part of a field to another. As you stand posed for your run-up, pause to feel the wind against your back and in your hair. Is it warm and gurgling with buoyant up-surges? Is it a slicing wind that can drive the disc

to the ground, or is it a tumbling wind that can just as easily drop a disc as shoot it forward? Should you shoot low and hard, or should you try to shelf the disc? If you start the first step of your run-up now, will you catch the next pulse of wind? That's the fun of outdoor distance—every throw is unique and incomparable, a blending of the forces of nature and the forces of your body at one time in one place as expressed by the flight of the Frisbee.

You're not likely to hit 413 feet on native strength, so there's not much point in aiming for it. Imagine instead a window out in the sky that represents the point where you are going to deliver your throw over to the winds. Estimate the window so that, if you get the disc through it with the most appropriate attitude on it, you can count on the wind giving the disc the longest possible carry. After each throw ask yourself: should the window be

The "macho sidewinder," Victor Malafronte's sidearm distance throw, is shown here at less than full power. The spread of the fingers in the grip and the fact that he looks straight ahead during delivery indicate that he is throwing for accuracy as well as distance. The lack of complete follow-through in the nonthrowing arm in the last figure is another indication that accuracy was an important consideration in this throw.

higher than I thought? more to the right? should I get the disc there with a little more hyzer on it? with the nose lower? did that early fade mean that there are cross currents downfield? and so on.

I got my education on the fine points of distance throwing when Victor Malafronte visited me in 1975. I took him to the traditional distance range on campus, a grassy mall flanked on both sides by large oaks. A statue of Winged Victory with arms uplifted and wings outstretched presents a tempting symbolic target almost exactly one hundred yards downfield. I had seen scores of throws start hopefully down toward Victory, but none had ever covered much more than three-fourths of the distance. I was curious to see how Victor, one of the very few players at that time who had thrown farther than one hundred yards, would do.

We always threw from dead center between the trees, the better to stay away from the branches close in on either side. Many promising tosses had had their flights halted prematurely in those branches. Victor went instead to the right side of the field and rifled a sidearm that hugged close to the tree limbs all the way until it slammed into the wall that crosses the field at Victory's back—the first hundred-yard throw I had ever seen. He explained to me that he had thrown from that side of the field because the breeze, the way it was blowing that day, would catch that row of trees and be moving faster there.

Next, he moved up five yards, a plain case of cheating to me. But Victor explained that it was only a matter of getting his Frisbee to the wall eight or ten feet higher up so that it could catch the mass of air that was piling up over the wall and ride it for extra yards. What mass of air? I couldn't see it, but then it suddenly made sense. If wind is moving downfield, what else could it do when it got to the wall but gush over it. Victor's next throw sailed several feet over the wall.

"Now," he said, "I'll put one through her arms." Victory's arms spread only eight feet apart—a very small target for a throw that would have to cover at least 110 yards if it was to have enough height to get over the statue. Victor let fly with three more throws, still hugging the trees on the right side. But this time the disc faded back to the left near the end. Two steered right through Victory's arms; the other passed just to one side.

Victor is very talented in the physical side of distance throwing for certain, but that performance clearly owed a greater debt to his knowledge of the wind. I didn't realize until much later that he had never aimed at Victory. He had sized up the wind conditions with his first two throws and had simply aimed for the spot where he knew the wind would take over and do the rest.

10. Catches

There is no catching in golf and no trick catching in guts or ultimate, so the remainder of this book pertains almost entirely to freestyle play alone. And perhaps the single best way to improve your freestyle catching is not to think of it as catching at all—at least not as the simple act of grasping the disc. Catching in freestyle is a process. You judge the disc's flight as you set up to make your catch. You time whatever movement you make to the approach of the disc. Usually, you move your hand and arm with the disc in ways that minimize the effects of the disc's speed and rotation. The catch is not complete even after you clamp your fingers down at the instant of contact—the disc will continue for a moment to exert forces in your hand because of its speed and spin. These forces are best arrested when absorbed into the continuing motion of your hand and arm rather than when resisted only with the grip of the fingers and thumb. All this movement ought to blend into the cocking and throwing motions of your return throw. Think of

The thumb-up position of the hand is usually employed for catches in the chest region and below. If the disc about to be caught here has right spin on it, it can readily be shifted in the hand to a backhand grip. With left spin on it, it can readily be shifted to a side-arm grip.

The thumb-down position of the hand is generally employed for catches in the chest region and up. However, that doesn't always hold true, as in this hand-stand catch. Thumb-down catches yield overhand and hook-thumb grips.

catching as beginning with your partner's follow through and continuing through your own.

It has generally been concluded in Frisbee that all catches fall into two categories—the thumb-up catch and the thumb-down catch—but that is not quite the case. There are a small number of oddball catches, such as the fig. More important, however,

95

the spin of the disc makes for a number of subvariations of thumb-up and thumb-down catches. Take a disc and set it up (chapter 13) several times with both left and right spin, both rightside-up and upside-down. Make right- and left-handed thumb-up and thumb-down catches. Notice that on a

The fig is an example of one of a few limited-use, rarely seen, special-purpose catches. Its own special purpose is to gain an inch or so of reach for high btb catches. When the disc makes contact with the two raised fingers, bring the thumb up and in against the cheek.

right-handed thumb-up catch, for instance, with right spin you end up with a backhand grip; with left spin you end up with a grip that can be easily modified to a sidearm grip, if it isn't already a sidearm grip. The same is true for thumb-down catches —they produce both overhand and hook-thumb grips. While you're at it, try making a few catches in such a way that you end up with a thumber grip. Notice also the adjustments your hand makes in catching upside-down discs. Discs are no more difficult to catch when they arrive upside-down; it's the novelty that throws you.

Many trick catches put your hand in a fixed position in the path of the disc or even necessitate moving your hand toward the oncoming disc. However, you should avoid such "dead hand" catches when they are not part of a trick catch. They are simply a race to close your fingers on the disc before it can bounce out of your hand. Catches made so that the spin rolls the disc from the web of the hand into the palm (backhand grip and overhand grip) use much more surface area of the hand. Therefore, they are trustier than those in which the spin twists the disc away from the palm (hook-thumb grip and sidearm grip).

The last thing you want to do is try to figure out the appropriate thumb-up or thumb-down right- or left-handed catch each time your partner sends the disc spinning your way. That sort of concentration interferes with physical skill learning, which takes place on a subconscious level. You would probably end up dropping more and learning less. However,

Reach your hand behind you and make a quarter turn to execute a btb catch. Spread your hand wide, as here, to present maximum catching surface to the disc.

THE RULE OF THUMB

True catches, as mentioned in the introduction, are made in the "C" of the hand, between the fingers and the thumb. And, as mentioned in this chapter, catches vary depending on the spin of the disc and the position of the hand. Getting accustomed to the relationship between spin and hand position is a process that takes weeks or months. Here is a drill that may help you understand that relationship in an hour or two. Try it when you and your partner can deliver a variety of throws.

When your partner throws you the disc, call out its spin, "right" or "left." At the same time, turn your thumbs in the direction you call. For instance, with left spin (a) turn you hands so that both thumbs are to the left (a). Either hand will make a fan-grip catch. The left hand will end up in a backhand grip and the right hand in an owf grip. The whole process is similar for right spin (b).

Now, to catch so that you end up with a two-finger grip, turn your hands into position with the thumbs pointing in the direction opposite the spin. So, if the disc arrives with right spin, turn your thumbs to the left. Your left hand will end up in a sidearm grip and your right hand in a hook-thumb grip.

Fan-grip catches use more surface area of the hand and so tend to be trustiest. Catches made working with the spin, whether fan-grip or two-finger, are trustier than catches made fighting the spin, though, of course, you can catch against the spin (catching a left-spinning disc with a right-handed backhand grip, for example).

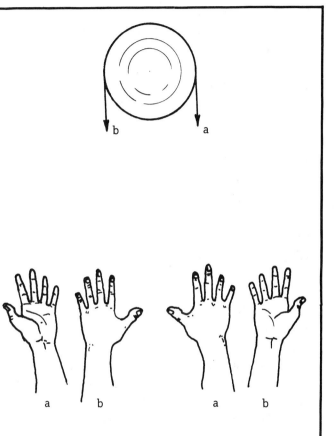

You just have to resist the spin and be quicker on the grip. Work on making catches with your hands in every possible position. Add to this the drill from chapter 5 on switching grips. How fluid your freestyle play is depends more than anything on how smooth you are between catch and throw.

if you are learning a new trick catch or are having problems with too many drops on an old one, get your partner to feed you several throws with each spin. If you prefer one spin over the other, have your partner feed you several more throws with that spin until you learn to automatically associate the catch with a particular throw.

You will miss out on a lot in Frisbee, incidentally, if you rely heavily on only one hand, particularly when you start to incorporate discwork into your play. Learn to use your nonpreferred hand now.

There are as many different trick catches as there are nicks in last year's Frisbee. This chapter and the next two present the basics, but you need to keep in mind that any catch presented here can usually also be performed while running, jumping, kneeling, squatting, twirling, stooping, and so forth. Play spontaneously and with imagination; keep your mind alert for new twists to add to the catches in your repertory.

The first trick catch most players try is the btb (behind-the-back) catch. Set up so that the disc approaches your offside at waist level. As the disc closes in, reach behind your back while you make a quarter twist to expose your catching hand. Keep your eye on the disc over your shoulder. Anticipating the catch by reaching behind your back too soon should be avoided; it limits your ability to adjust to the disc's flight. Until recently, btb catches were made almost exclusively with thumb-up catches. Thumb-down catches in the btb position require much more dexterity, but they can be very lovely, and they offer the advantage of putting you in position to return an overhand wrist flip. For a btb catch of a hover, try reaching beneath the disc and grasping it by the far edge. Again, you are in position for an owf return, even more so because the disc is already locked on your forearm.

When the disc arrives just out of reach of a leaping btb catch, it is at the right height for a bth

Thumb-down btb catches can be rather tricky, but they lend themselves to a variety of graceful catching moves. Most thumb-down btb catches must be made with the back well arched because of the difficulty in rotating the hand over into a level position otherwise.

(behind-the-head) catch. You will find nothing particularly difficult about bth catches—simply hold your hand up behind your head, then tuck your head out of the way when the disc gets there —but they certainly have a way of impressing on-lookers. Again, avoid anticipating the catch. For an effective fake move, reach for the disc with the noncatching hand, dropping your arm at the last instant or holding it just beneath the path of the disc.

The most versatile trick catches are the btl (be-tween-the-legs) catches. Try them facing forward, facing backward, leaping, kicking, charging, pivot-ing, squatting, one-handed, two-handed, thumb-up, thumb-down, every combination of these and any others you can think of.

A bth catch about to be made. Simply tuck the head out of the way at the last moment, but keep your eyes on the disc until you do.

Two-handed btl catches are a bit more tricky than many of the one-handed versions because of the nec-essarily stooped position. The problem of what to do with the disc once it is caught in this position de-mands resourcefulness. One clever recovery is to flip a butterfly back up through the legs.

One of the first catches to really shake freestyle loose from the toss-catch mental set of ball sports was the blind catch. The uninitiated observer is terrifically impressed to see a catch made in a stooped position where vision obviously can have little to do with successful performance. There are numerous blind catches, but the one in which you bow beneath the disc and make the catch over your back is still referred to as the blind catch. Try this catch first by setting yourself up with short boomerangs. Lean forward until your back parallels the angle of the incoming disc, keep your eyes on the

This dramatic cousin of btl and btb catches is the under-the-leg catch.

Trick catches take on new meaning when performed on a bicycle, particularly when, as above, they are attempted while riding across the grain of the flight.

Hovering throws, though, are easily jockeyed under. In fact, you can do very long TP&C's (throw, pedal, & catch).

disc as long as you conveniently can, and make the catch behind your back with both hands. When you can handle banked flights, start working with your partner on level flights.

The most common difficulty beginners encounter with the blind catch is the inability to get their hands quickly into the correct catching position. You and your partner can help each other here. One of you assumes the catching posture while the other checks the position of the hands. The hands should be raised above the back—thumbs down, fingers spread and pointed skyward—so that the tips of the thumbs are positioned about five centimeters higher than the highest part of your back. The palms should be turned outward so that they present the maximum catching surface to the disc. The webs of the thumbs should not be spaced wid-

With so many possible ways to make btl catches, you hardly need to make the same catch twice. Most btl catches are made as shown here with the back to the disc because the body and, particularly, the arms are left with more mobility than is the case in facing-stance btl catches.

The classic blind catch. Notice that the fingers point upward, the palms forward, and the thumbs downward. Learning to get your hands quickly into that position assures success with this catch.

er apart than the width of your disc. Hold the position a moment, then stand erect. Work on learning the correct hand position in this manner, then practice the catch with your partner walking the disc to you. Remember to keep your eyes on the disc as long as possible.

Work at first with throws that are headed for the pit of your chest. After a while, you can start going for those that are low by squatting and those that are high by stretching or leaping. When you are proficient, you will find the catch just as easy with one hand as two. When you really have this catch down, try making it while intercepting the disc across the grain of its flight.

An extra half twist or so added to a btb or bth catch produces a very graceful blind catch. For a bit of flash try two-handed grabs on btb and bth

With practice you will find the blind catch just as easy with one hand as two. Master practitioners of the one-handed blind catch often use their noncatching hand to distract attention from the catch. A quick tug on a sagging sock can leave onlookers wondering when and how the catch was made.

blind catches, one hand on either side of the body or both hands on one side. Try charging the disc at an oblique angle, leaping to a blind straddle with a two-handed btl catch.

Cross-body blind catches require extraordinary catching ability and timing. You should be proficient with the other blind catches before attempting to learn these or you may simply be undertaking an exercise in frustration. Not only do you move to a blind position relatively earlier in the flight of the disc, you also in many cases make large adjustments in the position of your hand while facing away from the disc. In the step-across cross-body blind, for instance, your hand sweeps

To turn btb and bth catches into blind catches, simply pivot earlier and further.

Mouth catches are best left to man's best friend, though Irv Kalb brought a crowd at the World Frisbee Championships to its feet with his mouth catch of an intolerable delay (chapter 14). Many dogs play a good game of Frisbee (though a little slack in throwing ability). However, if you don't break your furry partner of the common canine tendency to gnaw the disc as it is trotted back to you, you will need either to open a credit account with Wham-O or get used to the sensation that you are throwing a motorized rotary cheese-grater.

through an arc of about four meters before it returns to the catching position. Proper execution of these catches requires precise estimation of the disc's point of intersection with the plane of your body, but the beauty of these catches lies in the seeming unconcern for the disc's position that you display by taking your attention off the disc for so long. However, you are likely to find that, when you perform a cross-body blind, your accomplishment does not really register with casual observers; it is too alien to their experience.

Cross-body blinds fall into three categories: step-in, step-away, and step-across. The step-in is performed while reaching for the disc to your onside. Pivot on your onside foot or leap with your offside foot into your extended arm. Time your pivot so that your chest meets your arm just as the disc reaches your hand. Let the continuing motion of your body carry your arm on around through a full pivot. A three-arm backhand makes an outstanding return throw; in fact, the maneuver ought to be called a four-arm.

Set up so that the disc is headed to your offside for the step-away. Pivot to your rear on your offside foot, drawing your arm with you and folding it across your chest. Or, if the disc is headed to your onside, take a cross-over step with your offside leg. You need to displace your body on the pivot enough to move completely to the far side of the disc so that you have room to make the catch without the disc first hitting your back. Develop a uniform pivot at the outset—one for over-the-shoulder catches and one for catches made at chest level and lower. As you learn to make this catch consistently you can begin to vary your pivot.

Three different cross-body blind catches—the step-in, step-away, and step-across (top to bottom). The step-in catch is shown in its two-handed version, and the other two catches are shown with a three-arm throw for the return. The disc is shown telescoping in to point up the need to get all the way across the disc on the pivot.

The step-across cross-body blind is similar in that you set up with the disc to the offside and pivot on the offside foot. However, you pivot forward across the path of the disc rather than away from it. If the disc comes in to your onside, make your pivot by taking a cross step behind you with your offside leg. This catch, when the arm is extended, takes the hand from more than four feet on one side of the disc to more than four feet on the other side and then on around five feet for the catch—a flamboyant build up, so make the catch count.

An over-the-shoulder cross-body catch.

The supercharged instant of the disc's arrival is not the time for trying out intricate new moves. Learn the cross-body blinds one at a time. Have your partner walk the disc to you while you go through your moves. In the absence of a partner, place a disc on a table, make your pivot or cross step, then check to see if you have lined your hand up with the disc. Repeat the exercise with tables and shelves of various heights. Walk through the catch ten or more times before trying it with a flying disc. During play, if you balk a couple of times on the catch, stop and walk through it again. Get each new trick catch to the point that you do it automatically and consistently before taking on the next new one.

When you have all the trick catches down pat, when your game is so flawless it bores you, when you need a real challenge, take up stork (after Dan "The Stork" Roddick) catches. Incredible suppleness and the ability to dislocate joints at will are necessary. Simply wrap your arm once or twice around your leg or back or any other similarly inconvenient portion of your anatomy until it is about as mobile as a brick in a vice. Then flop over on your back or perch precariously on one toe. Catch the Frisbee.

A btb stork catch as performed by "The Stork" himself. Stork (constorksion) catches rob your arm of its mobility and so require you to make precisely timed moves of the body. In the first photograph the back-flop must be exactly timed to the flight of the disc, and in the other two the hand is left with not much more than its wrist motion to make a trailing-edge catch.

11. Trails

Trailing edge catches, or, as they are also called, trails, are those catches in which you follow the disc with your hand as it passes you, making the catch on the tail of the disc, usually when the tail is about even with the plane of the body. Trails add grace to any freestyle play and also liven the tempo because the catch puts your arm in the cocked position, ready for a quick return. You may find it tricky at first to let the disc head past you before you begin to make your catch, but you will overcome your tendency to reach early for the nose of the disc after a dozen or so tries. It's the seeming hesitation to make the catch that makes trails so intriguing to observers—the longer you hold off before making your catching move and the further behind you that you do make your catch, the more you will astound your audience.

You and your partner will need to set each other up with slow, steady feeders. Alertness to spin is critical to successful trails, particularly the onside trails, which require exceptionally precise contact with the disc. Explore the effects of spin on the

A btl trail. Notice, with the disc already moving past her, how far her hand still is from the disc. Trails are prettiest when the catch is made well behind the plane of the body.

various trails. Some you will find easier with normal spin, some with reverse. Others you may find equally easy with either spin, but the spin may determine your return throw. For instance, on a strangler trail (cross-body over-the-shoulder) with the roll shoulder near you, you could easily return a staker; with the skip shoulder to you, you might prefer after the catch to turn your wrist over and return an upside-down wrist flip.

The first trail to practice is the cross-body. Set up so that your partner's throw will pass just to your offside within about a foot above or below your waist. When the disc is about an arm's length from you, swing your arm around behind it. Time your catch—make it just as the tail of the disc breaks past the plane of the body. Return a backhand or a three-arm.

Next, try strangler trails and btl trails. You make the strangler by reaching for the disc over your offside shoulder. As already mentioned, you can return a staker or an upside-down wrist flip (let the spin determine which), though both are all but impossible at longer ranges. To increase the range of your return throw, bring your offside foot back as you make your catch so that you can throw from a closed stance rather than from a facing stance.

Between-the-leg trails are easiest with one leg kicked up. Otherwise, the lower the disc arrives, the easier the catch. What makes the catch easier in both cases is getting your upper body out of an upright position as much as possible so that it can twist or dip to add reach to the arm.

One of the flashiest moves in Frisbee is the return of a backhand pull immediately after a btl

An onside over-the-shoulder trail. Leaning backward lengthens the effective space you have to make your catch. A thumber from this position is one possibility for a quick return, but more common would be a turn into the catch to a blind stance with a two-arm wrist flip for the return. Or clap the disc to your back and lean forward for a backslide (chapter 15).

As soon as the catch is made in this btl position, the disc can be whipped forward for the return of a backhand pull.

trail. I have movie footage of Victor Malafronte performing this trick. Victor moves from an upright position to the catch (reaching so far behind himself that even his elbow extends out well behind his legs), makes the throw, and returns to an upright position in the course of fourteen frames (the film was shot at eighteen frames a second).

A tendency to knock the disc off its course before the catch can be made plagues the learner of the onside trail. To minimize that tendency, either lean forward and extend the hand straight back after the disc rather than allow it to swing back in an arc or, as shown here, make the catch halfway between the tail and the outside shoulder.

Only one of those fourteen frames shows Victor with the disc actually in his hand, which means that not more than one ninth of a second could have lapsed between the catch and the release of the return throw.

A sweep is an onside trail made with the arm fully extended. Set up so that the disc arrives an arm's length from your onside approximately shoulder high. If you start your arm after the disc from dead still, you will more often than not never even touch the disc. Either start your catching move by throwing your shoulder back to give your arm momentum to build on, or give your arm a push with your noncatching hand. Sweeps are the only trails that lend themselves well to practice off a set up; you may do well to try a few that way, using both spins, before heading off to the playing field.

The other onside trails are the over-the-shoulder,

made with the thumb down, and the below-the-shoulder (referred to simply as the onside trail), made with the thumb up. The first lends itself most readily to the return of a thumber or hook thumber, the second to an underhand return. An over-the-shoulder onside trail can be made with the thumb up, and that position has the virtue of allowing the return of a shoulder air bounce as well as of being a novel catch.

Except for the sweep, onside trails are less showy than their cross-body counterparts, because the arm movement is more restricted. However, the onside trails are quite a bit more difficult. Because the elbow must remain appreciably bent, the pendulum motion of the arm during the catching move is much shortened. So there is only a very brief range in which your hand will be moving level with the disc at contact rather than down or up on it. You can increase the range for making level contact with the disc on over-the-shoulder onside trails by leaning backward with the arrival of the disc and on waist-level onside trails by leaning backward or forward.

The forerunners of trails were catches made when the disc passed just out of reach, requiring the catcher to turn and run it down. A number of interesting moves have been refined from those old chase-down trails. One player I know does an overhead tunnel (chapter 15), then pivots and lunges after the disc to make the catch. Stancil Johnson, in his book, mentions the "Clarkerina" in his sec-

A two-handed overhead trail is an example of a catch that is not made easier by the use of both hands.

The extra catching hand is offset because you can no longer turn your upper body to get extra reach.

tion on trail catches. It is made by turning your back to the thrower, then snagging the disc as it passes.

Numerous other trails exist (and remain to be discovered). You can execute trails behind the back, under the legs, backward between the legs, and behind the head. With trails being such a varied and demanding class of catches, let me join Roy Rogers in wishing "happy trails to you."

Begin the sweep by giving your arm a push with your free hand. Try to make con- tact with the disc square on the tail just as your arm passes being even with your shoulders. If you continue to coil around after the catch, you end up in position to re- turn an owf or, as shown here, an owf air bounce.

12. Traps & Freezes

Do you remember how you caught the first Frisbee ever thrown to you? More than likely you used a sandwich trap, clapping your hands together with the disc in between. Even veteran Frisbee players, when startled by the unexpected arrival of a disc, often make an automatic sandwich trap. It is apparently the catch Nature intended us to make, yet it is so blah it's not worth using in freestyle. It does get a lot of use in ultimate, but even there it has the drawback of requiring adjustment of the grip before a pass can be readied.

The trick to a successful knee trap is to get one knee up over the disc.

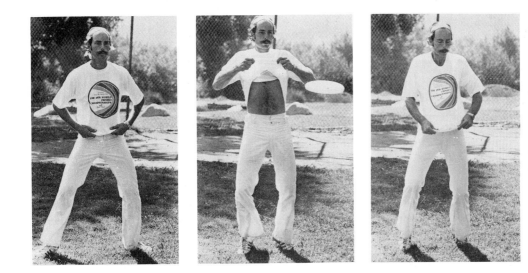

The shirt trap offers a chance to display a little Frisbee sleight of hand. However, let the expression on his face in the last frame stand as a warning not to use this catch for guts throws.

As many traps exist as there are parts of the body that can touch together, and then some. A trap is a catch made by wedging the disc between any two parts of the body other than the thumb and fingers. Freezes are traps made on the rim of the disc. Most traps require a good deal of imagination, co-ordination, and body movement, and so they are a lot of fun. In freestyle routines, however, they are used only sparingly because (with a couple of noteworthy exceptions that will be mentioned in this chapter) they tend to disrupt the rhythm of exchanges. Use traps in your freestyle routine to cap off a string of electrifying exchanges or a brilliant piece of discwork in order to give the audience time to catch its breath and ponder what you've done.

For the player with imagination there are an unlimited number of traps. Even the mundane sandwich trap (which is also known, incidentally, as the hamburger catch and as the clap-trap) has some variations which, if not altogether worthwhile, are at least curious enough to merit use now and then. Use a trailing edge sandwich trap with the return of a sandwich throw in close-range freestyle, or make the catch with only your fingertips and return a double spider. One-finger sandwiches defy success. Even on the rare occasions when your two fingers meet perfectly, the disc usually manages to get away. However, you might have better luck using a one-finger sandwich on an intolerable delay, or, again, on a delay, you can trap with your free hand to set up a scoop (chapter 15).

The leg trap. Once the catch is made, you must either get your feet back under you to land in a squatting position, remove the Frisbee with your hand and land standing, or land on one leg.

of the disc with a hand or finger as it lands on your head, is a favorite with very young audiences, particularly when followed by slap brushing the disc off your head back to your partner.

Leg traps have proven more important in freestyle than arm traps have, obviously because of the oddity of catching anything with the legs, but also because leg traps require great leaping moves and a fair degree of dexterity. A knee trap, for example, has to be performed in mid-air so that the legs are free to move toward each other. The trick is to raise one knee up over the disc. You'll find after a little practice that the knee trap works consistently, much more so than seems possible.

To set up for a forearm trap, position your arms out in front of you, folded hand to elbow. Spread your forearms apart enough to allow the disc room to pass between, and, as it does pass between, clamp your forearms together. There are obviously many possible positions in which you can make a trap between a hand or an arm and another part of the body. The blind catch, for instance, often ends up as a back trap. The only other arm traps I'll mention are the underarm trap and the head trap; the others I'll leave to your imagination. Complete the underarm trap by raising your arm up over the disc and bringing it down to lock the disc against your side. The head trap, which is simply the trap

An ankle trap is the preferred catch when overtaking a roller. Leap up high enough to bring your weight down full on your feet rather than let your momentum continue forward or you'll end up bunny hopping across the field. With a little extra effort you can kick the disc all the way over your shoulder.

The ankle trap is one of the noteworthy exceptions I mentioned above. Its value in freestyle comes from the fact that you can get the disc back in play by kicking it up in front of you or, more easily, behind you after you have it between your ankles. That feature makes it very useful for catching rollers, particularly ones you chase down from behind. Try to trap the disc and kick it back up without a pause between the two moves. Of course, leaping catches are also possible, but try to avoid landing on your Frisbee. Not only is it possible to crease or break your disc, but, if you are playing on pavement or wood, it's possible to take a bad fall. (Similarly, you should avoid stepping on a disc while running. It will usually scoot out from under you leaving you headed for a crash.) Leaping ankle traps with a kick up of the disc before landing have been successfully performed on occasion, but much more usual is a kick up after landing. If you like acrobatics, try making an ankle trap as you tumble over onto your back.

The last of the basic leg traps is one made by turning your back to the disc and trapping it between thigh and calf of one or both legs. It's a simple enough catch if made by squatting down on the incoming disc, but, if made while leaping, landing with legs doubled up can be a problem.

Flats are catches you can make when the disc has little or no spin left. Simply let the disc land flat on your plam, your outstretched forearms, or your back. Follow the catches with a pizza throw or scoop (palm), a drop to a squatting btl catch or a slight flip to set up an air brush (forearms), or a backslide (back).

Set up for a freeze by spreading your hands apart the width of the disc you are to catch (width varies from model to model). When the disc makes contact with your hands, press lightly against the rim to trap the disc. Whether you attempt the freeze with fingers pointed up, down, or straight ahead, tilt your hands slightly inward to make a

The freeze requires a light touch. Too much pressure or uneven pressure can cause the disc to squirm out of your hands. Angle your hands in a little to give yourself some margin for error in judging the width of the disc.

When the disc you are working starts to lose its spin, cradle it in a cross-armed freeze and set it up by flinging your arms apart. The direction of the spin you impart depends on which way you cross your arms. Left over right produces left spin, right over left, right spin.

"V" shape pointed back toward you. You can freeze the disc by its nose and tail as well as by its shoulders, and you can execute freezes behind the back, between the legs, with your forearms, with your legs, and whatever other ways your imagination leads you to.

An inside freeze is made by pressing outward against the inside rim of the Frisbee. The catch is usually made using the forefinger of each hand, which puts you in position to deliver a two-finger catapult. When the catch is attempted on a right-side-up disc, the disc must be virtually dead (without spin), but, for some reason, an upside-down disc can be caught with a modest amount of spin on it.

The other trap noteworthy for its use in free-style play is the cross-armed freeze. It comes in two versions: one, with fingers pointed upward, is for catching dropping discs from beneath; the other, the inverted cross-armed freeze with fingers pointed downward, is for catching dropping discs by diving on them from above. With either version the disc can be set up by flinging the arms outward. Both versions are valuable in discwork because they can add spin to a disc and because they offer just about the only graceful way to change the direction of spin on a disc.

The inverted cross-armed freeze on a dropping disc followed by a set up with left spin.

13. Tips

Frisbee shattered the three-million-year-old rigid human conception of throwing and catching in little more than twenty years. Still, throwing and catching are recognizable territory. Frisbee has recently entered into a completely new frontier (not that the other areas have been so thoroughly mapped out that they have no surprises left to offer).

Discwork is that new frontier. It would not have been comprehensible in any earlier age because it requires a mind that is attuned to the Space Age.

Discwork is the manipulation of the disc's flight energy. To work the disc, a player must be aware of (but does not necessarily need to have an understanding of) the disc's physical and material features and the features of its flight. Of course, these many features are interconnected at several levels. The player must recognize at every instant the energy state of the disc in terms of its attitude, spin direction, direction of flight with respect to the wind, flight momentum, stability, lift, and so forth, and must also recognize what states the disc is

headed toward and how any desired state can be produced. When space shuttles whisk from planet to planet and galaxy to galaxy, who will be at the controls? Frisbee players, of course, because they have developed an intuitive feel for flight. In fact, it occurs to me that the controls of such a spaceship might very well be shaped like a Frisbee disc with a flexible shaft carrying electrical wires that transmit the pressure of the pilot's fingertips to the appropriate flight mechanisms.

As always in Frisbee, a light touch reveals most. A heavy-handed touch will scramble up the ingredients of the disc's flight as if they were the bits of glass in a kaleidoscope. With a light touch, you can get the patterns to repeat; you can begin to sense what the conditions of success are and to manipulate the disc with precision.

Three years ago, when discwork began to emerge from a miscellany of early techniques, it worked only with what I call "native spin," the energy the disc had when it arrived. Players were careful to conserve that energy so that discwork could be prolonged. When the energy dwindled, the disc was caught and thrown back to the partner. Soon, techniques came into being that could add spin (energy) to the disc. Others were discovered that could alter the disc's flight attitude. It was, of course, no longer important to conserve energy. The spin and motion of the disc could be reduced or even momentarily halted and then started up again. It is now entirely possible for one or more players to work the disc for hours without ever making a catch or throw.

Drill and rehearsal are essential, but a set, choreographed routine should only be an intermediate goal. The ultimate goal should be the development of creative awareness. A Frisbee disc in space at any energy state can be changed to any other energy state in a variety of ways. So far, not all changes (not even most) are humanly possible. But the potential is there. Players who have developed the ability to respond instantaneously, precisely, and inventively to the disc will continue to discover ways to work the disc.

Learning a set up is the first step toward learning discwork. A set up is a way of putting the disc up

Twirling the disc upside down.

A set up with left spin. The disc must be tossed up and spun sharply.

in the air with spin on it. An air-bounce set up was described in chapter 8 and an inverted set up was illustrated in the previous chapter, but the ordinary set up is made by placing your hands on the rim of the disc in the freeze position, turning your arms one way or the other until they cross, then uncrossing them sharply with a simultaneous upward toss.

The disc can be set up with right and left spin, rightside up and upside down. While set ups are handy for practicing catches, they are indispensible for practicing discwork.

The first bits of discwork most people learn are finger spin and the finger spinning catch, or, simply, finger catch. Finger spin is merely the twirling of the disc on your finger—not at all difficult. How-

A btb finger spinning catch.

ever, a little skill becomes necessary for alternating the fingers without disrupting the spin, for twirling the disc upside down, and for changing the attitude of the disc while keeping it twirling. A couple of quick twirls right before a sidearm delivery add flash. You can finish up a finger spin by flipping

To maintain the disc in a level attitude while tipping, the finger must move unerringly to the center of the disc.

Upside-down tips are springier than rightside-up tips and they also get a parachute effect that slows their upward motion sooner.

the disc off your finger to set up trick catches, brushes, and body rolls (see chapter 15).

The finger catch is made by gathering the disc in twirling on one finger. It can be mastered in a few attempts, particularly if you will lower your finger with the descent of the disc, letting it nestle onto your finger. Not all finger catches are as elementary. You may want to save learning the btb finger catch for advanced practice, and you may want to save trying a finger catch of a disc dropping upside down for last. It requires the utmost in precise contact with the disc.

A tip is made by striking the disc on the flight plate (top or bottom). Most often, you will use your middle or index finger. Sometimes, particular-

A cross-legged heel tip.

A heel tip.

Foot tips are extremely versatile. You can use almost any part of your foot and get the full range of tipped flights.

A head tip is best performed by making contact with the disc right at the hairline.

A knee tip.

ly when the disc has a lot of momentum, you might find it desirable at first to brace your tipping finger with your thumb or by crossing your fingers.

Multiple tips, you might guess, are made by striking the disc repeatedly. Back in the days of working only with native spin, multiple tipping contests were common. Irv Kalb did one hundred and forty-odd straight tips off one set up. If anyone ever beat that, I don't know about it.

You can use many parts of the hands besides the first two fingers: any of the other fingers or the thumb, the joint knuckles, the knuckles, a fist (at any angle), the heel of the hand, the back of the wrist, all the fingertips at once (bunched up or spread out), and the palm and fingers (known as a slap tip). The further from the center of the disc the tip is made, the more prolonged the contact of the hand with the disc, and the greater the surface area of the hand that touches the disc, the more the spin will be reduced. Slap tips and five-finger tips are used to kill the spin in order to set up scoops and other techniques that require a non-spinning disc.

Of even more interest than multiple tips made

only with the fingers are those made using different parts of the body in succession. The parts of the body commonly used are the top of the forehead, the elbow, the knee, the toe, the side of the foot, and the heel of the foot. Every now and then you can expect to encounter a nose tip, a shoulder tip, or some other rare species of tip. With a Mini-Frisbee you can even do a breath tip.

Tips can be used to change the disc's attitude. In fact, when the disc arrives with too much speed, the first tip is often used to give positive attitude to the flight in order to break the momentum. Such an initial tip is often called a break tip for that reason. The same physics are involved as in a

skip flight. If you make the tip along the radius from the center to the skip shoulder, the nose of the disc will come up. The more the break tip is made toward the radius from the center to the nose, the more the finger must be angled into the disc.

When a disc has no forward momentum, the physics of off-center tipping change somewhat. The disc will usually drop to the side it was tipped up on. You can practice by holding your nontipping arm out away from you at different angles as you tip. See what placement is necessary in the off-center tip to get the disc to glide down right into your outstretched hand.

Once you develop a feel for tipping, you can try tipping below eye level. All sorts of new possibili-

Multiple tipping begun with a set up and followed by a tip, an elbow tip, a knee tip, and a btb finger catch.

ties come into play: running with the disc, reaching around and between your legs, and changing back and forth from tips to delays.

Top tips require a very delicate touch. The slightest bit too much pressure can cause the disc to plummet like a ball. And, of course, when you reach over to tip the disc on the topside, the whole physics of the matter turns topsy-turvy too.

In fact, hitting downward on the roll shoulder produces similar results to hitting upward on the skip shoulder. You can use a top tip on the roll shoulder as a break tip.

Below-eye-level tipping requires a feel for the center of the disc.

You can make tips by reaching between the legs either **way and even by reaching behind the back.**

Working the disc from a kneeling position shows full confidence that the disc can **be kept under control.**

Tips can be carried on the run.

14. Delays

Delays involve keeping the disc spinning (not twirling) while balanced on the end of the finger. The technique probably evolved from the push tip, a tip made not by striking the disc, but by pushing it. In a push tip the disc, of course, spins briefly on the finger.

Most often, the disc rides on the fingernail or, sometimes, a callus on the fingertip. The plastic of a Frisbee disc has a haze to it that the nail bites into, causing excessive friction. Numerous players use such devices as sewing thimbles; guitar picks; sticks made of plastic, compressed fibers, wood, or other materials; and even custom-made rings to minimize the friction.

The recent introduction of lubrication to delays has reduced the necessity for other aids. There's no point in listing all the things you can smear on your disc to get longer delays. The product that has found most favor is Armor All, which is available through automotive supply stores. A few drops on the underside of the disc (or topside for upside-down delays) are all you need. A light sanding and steel wooling of the disc will also help give you friction-free delays.

To start out with though, your problem is to keep your finger near the center of the disc, and lubrication and other devices may not help there. The best learning aid I have heard of involves preparing a disc this way: submerge the disc in hot tap water, take it out and work the center of the underside with firm pressure from the thumb, then resubmerge it in cold water. This will raise a very slight dome in the center of the disc that will make it easier for you to keep your finger there.

An intolerable delay works with the native spin

A nail delay.

A disc can be delayed atop any number of objects, from twigs to thimbles, to specially prepared sticks.

of the disc until there is no stability left to keep the disc balanced. Working with a disc in the last stages of an intolerable delay is much trickier than working with a hard-spinning disc.

Delays are frequently used to change the attitude of the disc. The greater the change desired, the further from the center you must move your finger. Some attitude changes may require that you shift to a rim delay, letting your finger slide all the way to the cheek and holding the delay there with your fingernail riding in the crease between the cheek and the flight plate.

As your finger slides out to the cheek, you could also give a firm flick to catapult the disc to your partner or a light flick to set up brushing, body rolls, and other intricate maneuvers. A light flick can also flip the disc around behind the head or set

up pirouetting or blind catches. An obvious way to disengage the finger from the disc is simply to drop the finger out from under it. That can set up kick tips and other below-eye-level tips. You can use a push tip to disengage, or you can simply brush or tip the disc with your free hand. Perhaps the most

Photo by Victor Malafronte

The flying disc ring is available from Wizard Enterprises of Berkeley, California by custom order. The spindle is free-spinning to provide maximum control in contact with the cheek but with a minimum of friction.

Carrying the disc under the leg on a delay and disengaging it with a tip.

An upside-down delay.

spectacular way to disengage a delay is to touch the lip of the disc to your chest and let the disc roll out along your arm to your other hand.

If you have room to move your arm with the incoming disc, you can catch even rapidly moving discs in a delay. Simply start lifting upward as you find the center. Once you've got the delay going, you can carry the disc under your legs, behind your back, or to your co-oping partner, and you can use it to set up a multitude of discwork tricks. The delay is used to control the energy of the disc in a more constant fashion than is possible with other discwork techniques. For that reason, it is often used as the transition from one maneuver to the next, as well as making for some spectacular maneuvers of its own.

Carrying a delay on the run is very similar to carrying tips on the run. You can switch back and forth between delays and tips with ease.

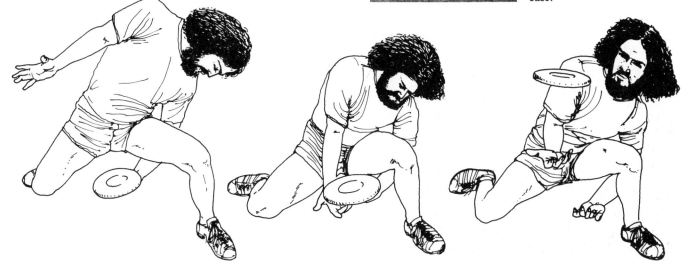

The only trouble is that there are eight delays, not one. A delay with right spin has a different feel from one with left spin. You need to learn to handle each spin with each hand and then to handle both rightside-up and upside-down delays.

There is, in fact, a ninth delay: the head delay. Every now and then, you can run under a disc and, by careful maneuvering of your body, get it to remain spinning on your head.

Padiddling is a technique somewhat related to delays. It involves building up the spin of the disc with rapid circular motions of your finger. Unlike a delay, however, the more friction, the better. In fact, padiddling is simple with something like a cafeteria tray, which is large, heavy, and rectangular (the odd shape gives a flywheel effect to keep the momentum going). A disc, on the other hand, is small, light, and circular, which makes padiddling much more difficult. Very fine movements are necessary. If you spend a little time every day working on a padiddle, you should find yourself getting the hang of it after two or three weeks. Some players can use a padiddle to work up a spin comparable to what can be obtained from a set up.

By rolling your finger just slightly, you can move from padiddle to delay and vice versa. However, you can get ejected from intolerable delay contests if you get caught padiddling.

A little-finger delay.

Rim delays are frequently used to set up air brushing.

One way to transfer a delay to your co-oping partner. José (bottom) and Châu (top) include incredible acrobatics in their freestyle. The question is, is José standing or kneeling?

15. Brushes & Scoops

To get an air brush, bat the disc gently up into the breeze with a glancing slap of the hand on the rim. The nose of the disc must be up; how much depends on the amount of breeze and the direction of the breeze relative to the direction the disc flies after the brush. Into the breeze, the disc can remain almost level; steeper **angles** are required as the

amount of lift provided by the breeze decreases. You can make slight adjustments in the disc's attitude, raising or lowering the nose, with a brush, but relatively large adjustments are best made during a succession of brushes. Brushes are also used to increase or decrease spin. With carefully controlled brushing, you can bring one spin down slow enough that you can impart the opposite spin with a slap in the other direction.

Vary the length the disc flies on each brush, alternate back and forth between both hands, brush the disc as you run; there are any number of things you can do with air brushes. For one thing, you can also brush with your leg or foot or even your back.

The air brush can be made with the full length of the hands or with only the fingertips.

Quite a bit of practice is necessary to be able to get as accurate a glancing blow with your foot as is possible with the hands, but foot brushes can be done with almost uncanny precision.

A thumb brush is a quick stroke of the thumb or fingers used to increase or decrease spin or to check the disc's forward momentum. The disc will drop fast, so thumb brushes are generally reserved for head-high throws, and the disc is picked up on a delay or with a below-eye-level tip after the brush.

Directionals, or guides, are similar to brushes except that the hand (or whatever) is held relatively still as a backboard for the disc to carom off of by virtue of its spin. The contact must come near the roll shoulder of the disc or the spin will be killed. The instep of the foot can be planted in the path of a roller to make the disc pop up to the catcher or even to make the disc roll up the leg.

An instep guide can pop a roller right into your hands.

A shoulder roll. This roll is sometimes used to set up a knee trap for the co-oping partner.

The steep angle of the arms in this chest roll indicates that the disc had little momentum on it.

Body rolls are directionals that involve continued contact with the disc. The disc can be rolled from one hand to the other across the chest or the back. A below-waist-level back roll is of course known as a parkerhouse roll. To get a smooth chest roll, turn your shoulders forward and sink your chest back to make as smooth a curve as you can.

Catching the incoming disc with a shoulder roll.

Once you can do a chest roll, try one with both you and your co-oping partner, so that the disc travels four arm lengths.

For successful body rolls, the roll shoulder (the one in contact with the body) must almost always be lower than the skip shoulder. Body rolls can be set up in a number of ways, many already mentioned, but the player must always be aware of the spin direction of the disc. Again, contact with the skip side of the disc can kill the spin.

Another technique sometimes used to set up body rolls is the flip out. Hook your fingers under the rim and flip the disc one direction or the other. A flip out doesn't put much spin on the disc, so you will need to make a downward roll path with your arms to take advantage of gravity.

The spin of the disc must be dead before the disc can be scooped. Scoops are performed by plac-

A flip out to a brush. Flip outs also come in very handy for getting rollers and gym-floor curves up from the ground.

ing the palm and fingers of your hand against the flight plate and swooshing the disc through the air. A scoop made on the belly is called a cheater scoop, because the fingertips can hug the cheek for surer control. Scoops can go behind the back or between the legs and can even be used to set up air brushes.

Scoops can also be used to begin a backslide. Clap the disc to the back, then straighten up some so that the disc slides down the back. Make a catch reaching back between the legs. Backslides can also be started with over-the-shoulder trails, and backslides can be angled across the back as well as down it.

Getting ready to fluff the disc.

A btb scoop can be used to set up a fluff, an upside-down finger catch, a btl catch, and any number of other tricks.

A backslide.

A tip made with one or both forearms is called a fluff. It is not quite a tip, because the arms strike the edge of the disc. Fluffs are very useful for making large changes in the disc's attitude, though they must be made quickly or they will slow the spin appreciably.

The forearms can also be used as a surface for skipping the disc, as can the leg, back, chest, and head. Simply touch your forearm to the skip edge of a good, brisk skip curve, and the disc will skip as if it had hit the ground. The friction of the skin is large, which means both the spin will be much reduced and that a scratched up disc will feel like a power sander. Some players have begun to wear a

A forearm skip followed by
a fluff and a back brush.
The disc settles down ready
for an air brush.

A break tip in co-oping,
with a tunnel to a btb catch.

plastic sleeve so that they can get forearm skips without these problems. You can also use a second disc held in your hand as the skipping surface (known as friz skips).

One discwork technique requires no contact with the disc at all. The object of tunnels, in fact, is to get close to the disc without touching it, although tunnels can be used as a mask for a directional now and then. To form a tunnel, just touch your fingertips together. To tunnel, just let the disc fly through your arms. Tunneling is essentially a co-oping maneuver, the exception being the occasions when a single player might use it on a dropping disc. Tunnels are most interesting when they are timed in with a pivot or even a pirouette. A tunnel made by stooping under an incoming disc is called a disco duck, of course.

An over-the-shoulder tunnel.

A btl tunnel.

16. Pick Ups

Your partner's right-handed sidearm banks in off the breeze to your left, and automatically you turn so that your left arm points into the breeze. You extend your right hand up to meet the disc. Intuitively, your left arm drops just a little, and your left hand tilts back slightly. The disc whizzes across your chest and flies from your left hand, nose up into the breeze. You race after the disc, batting its tail with brushes—right, left, right, left—each brush gets lighter until the disc seems to be dancing at the ends of your fingers. You reach under the disc for a brief delay. As your nail rides the spin of the disc forward and to the right, the nose of the disc comes further up. You flick your nail against the cheek, and the disc sets up—one more brush. What could cap off this moment but a leaping pirouette catch? You leap, and as you come full circle, you reach around for the disc with your hand. Even before your head has turned enough for you to see the

Pick ups take on an added dimension in mobile Frisbee. Pick ups in bicycle Frisbee are as fun as any other part of the game.

Step on the rim to get the disc to flip over onto your foot. Here the toe up is followed by a btb catch.

disc, you feel its impact—not in your hand, but against your knee. You look down, and the disc is lying inert on the ground. What do you do?

Ordinarily, you might reach down and pick the disc up. But this moment still demands something special. What you do in this instance depends on whether the disc lies rightside up or upside down.

If the disc landed rightside up, you can straddle it and freeze it between your feet. Then jump to kick the disc up behind you or to bring it up in front of you. You can also try a foot brush, but the success rate is low unless the disc happened to land

with one edge propped up slightly. You can also use one foot to shove the disc up on the other and then proceed with a toe up, lifting the disc with your foot.

If the disc is upside down, the possibilities multiply. Obviously, if you are barefooted, you can simply pick it up with your toes and throw it back. If you step down on the rim, the disc will flip over onto your foot, ready for a toe up (also known as a flip up kick up pick up when done in this manner). You can flip the disc up to the inside of your foot, then kick it up with an ankle trap as shown in chapter 12. With shoes on, you can simply catch your heel against the cheek and flip the disc up behind you.

A two-finger inside freeze pick up allows the return of a finger flip catapult.

For a surprise move, reach down and pick up the disc with your hand. Hook one finger on the cheek and hike the disc up over your head. With one finger you can also make a finger spinning pick up—once you are used to twirling the disc upside down.

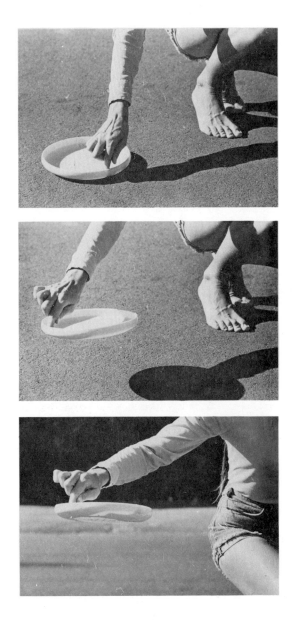

PHOTOGRAPH IDENTIFICATION KEY

Page 1—Tom Kennedy; p. 3—Roy Claus; p. 5—Tom McRann; p. 6—Tom Shepherd; p. 7—John Anthony; p. 12—Dan Roddick; p. 14—José Montalvo (left), Patti Hipsky.

Chapter 2: p. 42—Ed Headrick; p. 44—John Sappington; p. 45—Jon Bach (left), Jim Baumann; p. 47—Roy Claus; p. 49—Victor Malafronte.

Chapter 3: p. 53—Victor Malafronte; p. 54—Claire Parish; p. 55—Kerry Kolmar; p. 56—Gail McColl; p. 57—Jim Howard.

Chapter 4: p. 61—Rick Kauvar (left), Monika Lou (top right), Kerry Kolmar; p. 62—Author.

Chapter 5: p. 64—Roy Claus; p. 66—Mike Conger; p. 67—Kerry Kolmar (left), Marc Reischman.

Chapter 6: p. 69—Author (left), Tom Bodá; p. 70—Gail McColl; p. 72—Author.

Chapter 7: p. 73—Victor Malafronte; p. 75—Victor Malafronte.

Chapter 8: p. 80—Tom Monroe; p. 83—Jim Howard.

Chapter 9: p. 86—Danny McInnis, Don Grefe (watching); p. 87—Jim Howard, Don Grefe (watching).

Chapter 10: p. 95—Marvin Vitatoe (left), John Sappington; p. 96—Victor Malafronte; p. 98—Jeff Jorgenson; p. 99—Don Cain (left), Jens Velasquez; p. 100—Author (left), Ziggy King; p. 101—Jim Howard (top left), Mike Conger (bottom left), Jo Cahow; p. 102—Victor Malafronte (left), John

BOOKS OF RELATED INTEREST

SKATEBOARDING by Jack Grant is the first complete guide to this fad-turned-major-sport. Riding positions and major tricks are extensively illustrated and the concise text covers everything from fundamentals to safety. 112 pages, soft cover, $3.95

In THE WORLD OF WOMEN'S GYMNASTICS, Jim Gault and Jack Grant have written a stimulating, insightful, and extraordinarily instructional overview of the sport. Gymnasts, coaches, judges, parents, teachers, and enthusiastic spectators will all learn from it—and love it. 144 pages, soft cover, $3.95

PLAYING TENNIS WHEN IT HURTS is for the millions of tennis players who suffer minor orthopedic ailments. Dr. Kenneth G. Campbell helps the reader to identify and define his condition, gain insight into the mechanics of it, and work toward overcoming it while continuing to play. "There is no question that anybody who takes the time and trouble to follow (Dr. Campbell's) advice will find it worthwhile. . . a useful book." —Sports Illustrated 128 pages, soft cover, $4.95

Jerry Colletto's YOGA CONDITIONING AND FOOTBALL presents a revolutionary new approach to conditioning for athletes and general fitness for everyone. 112 pages, soft cover, $3.95

BICYCLE MOTOCROSS: A COMPLETE GUIDE by Ted Wise contains information on equipment, tracks, safety, tricks, jumps, sanctioning organizations, racing psychology, practice and maintenance for America's fastest growing new sport. 128 pages, soft cover, $3.95

In BEYOND JOGGING: The Innerspaces of Running, Michael Spino brings together spiritual concepts such as meditation and body awareness with the physical techniques of Oylmpic coaches to make running a creative, self-actualizing experience. ". . . After Mike Spino, running will never be the same. . ." —George Leonard 128 pages, soft cover, $3.95

In I AM NOT SPOCK, Leonard Nimoy reveals the experiences and adventures he shared with the legendary STAR TREK character he created—Mr. Spock, First Officer of the Starship Enterprise.
". . . a most intriguing voyage through inner space. . ."
—New York Times

". . . a remarkably pleasant and gentle tale of the only fictional character since Sherlock Holmes to have won the love of millions entirely by being rational. . ."
—Isaac Asimov

". . . I AM NOT SPOCK's openness, candor and wit will provide solid, enjoyable reading for any literate, regardless of age."

—Grover Sales

152 pages, soft cover, $4.95 Also available: Live Long and Prosper poster, 23" x 35", two color, $2.00

Available at your local book or department store or directly from the publisher. To order by mail, send check or money order to:

CELESTIAL ARTS
231 Adrian Road
Suite MPB
Millbrae, California 94030

Please include 50 cents for postage and handling. California residents add 6% sales tax.